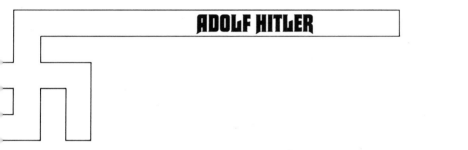

ADOLF HITLER

EILEEN HEYES

The Millbrook Press
Brookfield, Connecticut

Photographs courtesy of the National Archives: pp. 10, 25,
49, 52, 61, 86, 97, 104, 138; Bettmann Archive: pp. 14, 18;
Bundesarchiv, Koblenz: p. 28; Library of Congress: pp. 35,
38; UPI/Bettmann: pp. 42, 58, 63, 66, 74, 81, 118, 128;
AP/Wide World: pp. 71, 125; Yad Vashem, Jerusalem, Israel,
courtesy of the United States Holocaust Museum: p. 92;
Sovfoto: p. 108. Map by Joe LeMonnier.

Library of Congress Cataloging-in-Publication Data
Heyes, Eileen.
Adolf Hitler / Heyes, Eileen.
p.   cm.
Includes bibliographical references and index.
Summary: Presents the story of the German Nazi leader
in the context of the political and social forces of his time,
focusing on the destruction and misery he unleashed in
World War II and the Holocaust and examining as well
the legacy of his actions.
ISBN 1-56294-343-X (lib. bdg.)
1. Hitler, Adolf, 1889–1945—Juvenile literature.   2. Heads
of state—Germany—Biography—Juvenile literature.
3. National socialism—Juvenile literature.
4. Germany—History—1933–1945—Juvenile literature.
[1. Hitler, Adolf, 1889–1945.   2. Heads of state.
3. National socialism.   4. Germany—History—
1933–1945.]   I. Title.
DD247.H5H326 1994 943.086'092—dc20 [B] 93-31269 CIP AC

Published by The Millbrook Press
2 Old New Milford Road, Brookfield, Connecticut 06804

CONTENTS

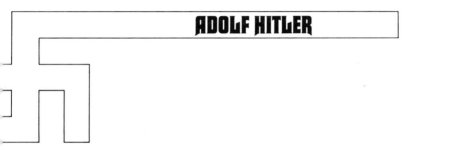

ADOLF HITLER

INTRODUCTION

THE NUMBERS ALONE TELL A LOT.

More than 12 million people were killed in concentration camps and death camps, 6 million of those because they were Jewish.

In all, 40 million Europeans died in a war that lasted less than six years. More than 17 percent of the population of Poland perished, more than 10 percent of the populations of the Soviet Union and Yugoslavia.

But the numbers don't tell it all. They don't tell of the shattered conscience of a nation, the broken lives, the human misery that spread like a field of poisonous mushrooms planted and nurtured by one man.

Racism, destruction, violence, death. These were all part of every day in Adolf

Adolf Hitler, about 1925. He led the forces that killed more than 12 million people because they were Jewish or considered either racially inferior or a political threat.

Hitler's Germany, and in the other sections of Europe that fell under his command.

When Adolf Hitler came to Germany, he was an aimless Austrian without education or trade. He was driven by twin racial views: that Germans belonged to a master race with an innate right to rule, and that Jews were vile subhumans on a campaign to capture the world for themselves.

With sure political instincts and a gift for captivating crowds, Hitler won followers and turned the Nazi party into a political powerhouse. He became chancellor of Germany on January 30, 1933, and Nazis began terrorizing the people almost immediately. By the following year, Hitler had become dictator. Germans were turned into prisoners in their own country. Jews were stripped of their civil rights, their property, their dignity, and finally their lives.

In 1939, Hitler started World War II, the most costly and destructive war the world has ever seen. As defeat loomed, he tried to destroy the German people, too.

How could one man do all this in a civilized, industrial nation in an era of mass communication? How could 70 million Germans let him do it?

The answers lie in the complex interaction between a unique personality and the political and social forces of his time. Some historians believe Hitler's rise was the culmination of centuries of German history; others blame short-term factors such as the tremendous political and social instability in Europe during Hitler's lifetime.

Any discussion of Hitler, therefore, must begin with a look at the nation that allowed itself to be led for twelve years by a mass murderer.

DEEP ROOTS. The political, social, and ideological currents that grew into tidal waves under the Nazis had existed for centuries. Militarism, obedience to authority, and anti-Semitism did not originate with Hitler.

The region we know today as Germany sits in the middle of Europe. Because of its location, the area has been invaded and trampled repeatedly over the centuries. Location also played an important part in Germany's downfall in World War I and would again in World War II, when German leaders had to fight on more than one battlefront at the same time.

Two thousand years ago, the region was occupied by warlike, pagan tribes. Once Christianity took root in Germany, the leadership of tribal warlords gave way to control by a collection of territorial rulers who also acted as religious leaders in their jurisdictions. Although the region in theory was bound under an emperor, in practice it remained fragmented. It consisted of more than three hundred individual states at the time central national governments were forming in Britain and France. While those nations developed a tradition of democracy during the eighteenth and nineteenth centuries, Germans still had their many authoritarian rulers.

Germany was the last of the great nations of Europe to be unified, and it was forged into one nation by military aggression. Otto von Bismarck, chancellor of the large and powerful kingdom of Prussia, launched a series of wars in the late nineteenth century to bring the other German states into one nation under Prussian domination. Significantly, Bismarck excluded Austria with its largely German population. Ending this separation of German peoples would become a major goal for Hitler.

Another concept central to Nazi rule was anti-Semitism, prejudice against Jews, which can be traced back for centuries. Throughout Western history, Jews have been persecuted. Since about the fourth century, they have been pressured to convert to Christianity, and some rulers have expelled Jews. The Catholic Church, which exercised tremendous power in Europe, enacted rules forbidding Christians to marry or have sex with Jews. It restricted education, employment, legal rights, and housing for Jews, and ordered them to wear identification badges. Secular rulers in Germany placed similar restrictions on Jews centuries before Hitler was born. During the Middle Ages, savage anti-Jewish terrorist campaigns, or pogroms, were launched in Germany and other parts of Europe. Jews were accused of causing a fourteenth-century plague called the Black Death. Martin Luther, the German monk who in the sixteenth century sparked the Protestant Reformation, characterized Jews as demons, archcriminals, and enemies of Christ; he said they should be stripped of their property and imprisoned or expelled.

With the exception of forced conversion, all of these measures—restrictions, identification badges, anti-Semitic propaganda, pogroms, expulsion, and imprisonment—were used by the Nazis to push European Jews toward the most terrible persecution the world had ever seen.

BENEATH THE SURFACE. Although Nazi doctrine had roots that went back many years, it was the upheaval in Europe during Hitler's lifetime that gave him a chance to gain power.

World War I (1914–1918) ended in a crushing defeat for Germany. Because the German Army

This engraving shows an attack on Jews in Frankfurt, Germany, in 1614. Anti-Semitism neither began nor ended with Hitler.

had kept tight control over information during the war, most people—including Adolf Hitler, then a soldier—were shocked to hear that Germany was about to surrender. A revolution in 1918 swept the Kaiser, Germany's ruler, from power, and he was succeeded by a government led by politicians who had not been involved in conducting the war. These civilians were the ones who, at the urging of military leaders, on June 28, 1919, signed the peace agreement that would contribute heavily to Hitler's success: the Treaty of Versailles.

Germans hated the treaty that had been forced on them by the victorious Allies (Britain, France, Russia, the United States, and several smaller nations). Under the treaty's provisions, Germany lost territory it had taken from France, Belgium, Denmark, and Poland and had to accept responsibility for starting the war. Germany was forced to pay huge reparations, or compensations for war damage, in gold, raw materials, livestock, and manufactured goods. The treaty cut German armed forces from several million men to 100,000, with no planes or tanks. People quickly forgot that the army had urged that the treaty be signed, and the "stab in the back" legend was born. The new civilian leaders, the story went, stabbed the army in the back just as it was about to win the war.

Because its constitution was drafted in the city of Weimar, the new democracy was known as the Weimar Republic. On paper, it was a progressive, liberal state. Germans were guaranteed freedom of speech, equality under the law, and inviolable personal liberty. Weimar Germany was the only European nation where women had the vote. The constitution was ratified on August 31, 1919, two months after the Treaty of Versailles was signed.

So, in the shadow of this widely despised treaty, and under the leadership of men believed to have sold out the mighty German Army, Germany's first democratic government came into being. Not surprisingly, it met resistance—from the army, from the judiciary, and from the public. With such a profound dearth of support, the Weimar government would prove unable to stand up to the powerful political and emotional forces unleashed by an undistinguished Austrian immigrant named Adolf Hitler.

"MOTHER'S DARLING"

1

Someone will have to come along
who thinks very simply. An uncultured
man, a peasant as it were, would solve
everything much more easily merely
because he would still be unspoiled.

He would also have the strength to
carry out his simple ideas.

HEINRICH TESSENOW
ARCHITECTURE PROFESSOR, 1931

Adolf Hitler is the little boy standing between his father and his beloved mother in this family portrait.

O N THE EVENING
of April 20, 1889, at an inn called the Gast-
hof zum Pommer in the village of Braunau
am Inn, Austria, the third wife of an Austrian customs official gave birth to a son. He
would be baptized and raised as a Catholic,
in the religion of his country. His name was
Adolf Hitler.

／Adolf's ancestors were small farmers
and craftsmen. The family name was spelled
various ways, including Hiedler, Huettler,
and Hitler. Adolf's father, Alois, was given
none of these names when he was born in
1837 to an unmarried peasant named Maria
Anna Schicklgruber. In later years, opponents of Adolf Hitler would try to claim that
his real name was Adolf Schicklgruber. But
since Alois Schicklgruber took his father's

name, Hitler, before Adolf was born, his son was legally entitled to this name from birth.

⁴Alois Schicklgruber joined the Austrian border patrol when he was eighteen, and he later became a customs official in Braunau am Inn. His first marriage broke up, and his second wife died of tuberculosis. In 1885, now using the name Hitler, he took his third wife, Klara Poelzl, the daughter of his cousin. Her family had lived on the same land in Spital, Austria, for four generations. She was already pregnant with Alois's child when they were wed. They had six children, but only Adolf and a younger sister, Paula, survived into adulthood. From his father's second marriage, Adolf Hitler had a half-sister, Angela, and a half-brother, Alois, Jr.

/ In his early school years, Adolf was, on the whole, a good student. He took singing lessons and sang in the choir at a Benedictine monastery. He found "the solemn splendor of the brilliant church festivals" intoxicating.¹ But his enthusiasm for learning and for the church didn't last. As adolescence dawned, he rebelled against his religious upbringing and rejected the career plans his father was making for him. Alois Hitler had attained the highest rank open to him in government service, and he was proud of his achievement. He wanted his son to become a civil servant, too. Adolf would have none of it. He fancied himself an artist and wanted to be a painter.

In fact, there was not much the willful young Adolf and his father agreed on. They argued often, and the domineering older Hitler criticized and sometimes even struck his son. Nonetheless, Adolf Hitler respected his father for having risen from humble beginnings.

Adolf Hitler was devoted to his mother and loved her deeply. He later recalled her as "giving all her being to the household, and [being] devoted above all to us children in eternal, loving care."[2] He thought of himself as "mother's darling," and he carried her picture with him.[3]

In 1900, Hitler entered a secondary school in Linz, Austria, where the Hitler family now lived. His academic prowess had vanished. In his first year he did so poorly that he was not promoted, and the dismal performance continued. Hitler later wrote that he had decided to simply stop working at any subject other than art in hopes that his father would let him pursue the career of his choice.

The dispute soon became moot. Alois Hitler died suddenly of a lung hemorrhage in 1903. Adolf Hitler, then thirteen, cried inconsolably when he saw his father's body. Two years later, Adolf himself suffered from a lung problem, and he talked his mother into letting him drop out of school. Yet he agonized over his decision, knowing how much it upset her.

That fall, in 1905, Hitler visited the country where he would one day become dictator. A pale, sickly looking teenager, he struck people who met him as shy and reserved. He spent a few months studying drawing in Munich, Germany, before he returned to Austria. For about two years, Hitler lived with his mother and kept himself busy sketching, painting, writing poems, and reading. He haunted libraries and surrounded himself with books. Sometimes he went to the opera or the theater with his only friend, August Kubizek.

The Austria in which Adolf Hitler grew up was beset by strife among immigrants. Prejudice against

Jews was one more source of ethnic conflict that was part of everyday life. By the time he reached his late teens, Hitler was already a vocal anti-Semite and a fanatic German nationalist. Although he was Austrian by birth, he considered himself German and believed the German-speaking peoples of Austria and Germany should be united in a single country. Furthermore, he firmly believed that he himself would one day receive a mandate from the people to lead them.

DISAPPOINTMENT SOWS SEEDS OF HATE. In October 1907, Hitler moved to Vienna, planning to attend the Academy of Fine Arts there. But his hopes were shattered when he took the entrance exam for the academy's school of painting. His test drawings were rated unsatisfactory, and he was not admitted. He had been confident of his ability, and later said the rejection "struck me as a bolt from the blue."[4]

According to Hitler's account, an academy official told him he could never make it as a painter and should study architecture. But getting into architectural school would have required a high school diploma or a demonstration of exceptional talent. Although he had been interested in architecture for some time, Hitler let the matter drop.

On the heels of the academy's rejection came tragedy: Hitler's beloved mother, Klara, died of breast cancer on December 21, 1907. Hitler had rushed home to care for her when he heard she was sick, and he was crushed by her death. He wrote that, even though he had known her illness was terminal, "it was a dreadful blow, particularly for me. I had honored my father, but my mother I had loved."[5]

Kubizek put it this way: "He had lost the only creature on earth on whom he had concentrated his love, and who had loved him in return."[6]

Hitler talked Kubizek into moving to Vienna, and the two shared a room there. Hitler pretended to be a student, living on a small pension and support from relatives. He continued reading industriously and made a habit of sitting in on sessions of the Austrian parliament. At night he ranted to his roommate about the sufferings of the German people and about what he already perceived as the Jewish problem. Although he lived and breathed politics, Hitler was not a joiner and did not associate with any existing political parties at the time.

In October 1908, while Kubizek was in Linz, Hitler tried again to get into the academy. This time his portfolio was judged as so poor that school officials saw no point in even letting him take the entrance exam. Leaving no word with Kubizek or his family, Hitler disappeared into the shadows of Vienna, where he tried, with little success, to peddle his paintings.

He worked on some small art projects, but within a year, twenty-year-old Adolf Hitler was flat broke. He had lost the room he had been renting. For a few days he panhandled for money and slept in cafes and on park benches. Then, in late 1909, he landed in a shelter for the destitute where he could get free soup. After a few months there, he moved to a slightly less seedy shelter called the Home for Men.

While he lived there, Hitler consumed newspapers hungrily, sometimes clutching two while reading a third. He would keep to himself and read or work on a painting until he overheard a comment about politics. Then he would leap up and harangue anyone within earshot, then abruptly stop, shrug, and return to his task. Hitler stayed for three years at the Home for Men, scratching out a living by selling paintings and wandering the streets among the dregs of Vienna. His family thought he was dead.

He later wrote: "In this period there took shape within me a world picture and a philosophy which became the granite foundation of all my acts."[7] Vienna teemed with immigrants and was plagued with poverty and overcrowding. Hitler was appalled at what he saw as the newcomers' disrespect for the Fatherland and the authority of the law. He concluded that left-wing activists were trying to stir up the oppressed masses and destroy the social order. At the far left on the political spectrum were Marxists, and Hitler began to hate them passionately. He claimed that this was also when his anti-Semitism crystallized.

Active anti-Semites in Vienna vented their hatred in various publications, some of them pornographic. The young Hitler echoed their views, blaming Jews for everything he disliked, from prostitution to modern art.

"In this period," he later wrote, "my eyes were opened to two menaces of which I had previously scarcely known the names, and whose terrible importance for the existence of the German people I certainly did not understand: Marxism and Jewry."[8] He became obsessed with Jews. "Once, as I was strolling through the Inner City, I suddenly encountered an apparition in a black caftan and black hair locks. Is this a Jew? was my first thought. . . . Wherever I went, I began to see Jews, and the more I saw, the more sharply they became distinguished in my eyes from the rest of humanity."[9]

Adolf Hitler poses with his fellow soldiers during World War I. The contacts he made in the army proved a stepping-stone to power.

A NEW CAREER. In mid-1913, Hitler moved to Munich, where again he barely managed to support himself as an artist. He had no friends, male or female. After three years of neglecting to get a physical for the Austrian military (as an Austrian citizen, he was required to get one), he finally did so in February 1914, only to be told he was too weak to be a soldier. But when World War I broke out in August, Hitler petitioned the German state of Bavaria for permission to serve in its army. He was accepted as a volunteer in the 16th Bavarian Reserve Infantry Regiment.

On the battlefield, the social misfit became the consummate warrior. Here, he felt at home. He never complained about the hardships of battle, a silence his fellow soldiers found odd. Hitler eventually became a corporal.

Working as a dispatch carrier for his regiment, Hitler showed himself to be a fearless soldier and was decorated twice for bravery. On August 4, 1918, he was awarded the Iron Cross first class, one of the highest awards a German soldier could win. That October, he was injured in a British gas attack. While he was in the hospital recovering, he got the stunning news that Germany had been defeated. Hitler felt empty and bereft. Not ready to let go of the fight, he went to work as a civilian employee of the District Army Command in Munich. Now he found a new fight: the army's struggle against the new government.

Many military leaders believed that the army had been betrayed by Germany's new civilian leaders, the signers of the Treaty of Versailles. These military men wanted nothing more than to see the Weimar democracy overthrown; Hitler shared this desire. The District Army Command put Hitler to work lecturing returning soldiers and looking into the many right-wing political groups popping up in Munich. He found that he had a talent for public speaking.

More important, it was in this job that the future dictator stumbled, quite by accident, onto the organization that would be his path to absolute and unchallenged power.

"THE FIREBRAND OF THE WORD"

All great movements are popular
movements, volcanic eruptions
of human passions and emotional
sentiments, stirred either by the
cruel Goddess of Distress or by
the firebrand of the word.

ADOLF HITLER
MEIN KAMPF

Hitler mesmerizes his newly organized paramilitary unit, the Nazi storm troopers.
Dressed in brown-shirted uniforms and
armed with guns and Hitler's rhetoric,
these young men resorted to violence at the
slightest provocation.

THEY MET IN A BACK room of the Sterneckerbräu beer hall, the men in this odd little band. They called themselves the German Workers' party, although there were only a few of them. Founded by a locksmith and a sportswriter, the group had its roots in anti-Semitic and German expansionist movements dating from the nineteenth century. On September 12, 1919, a pale, thin veteran with a close-cropped mustache and a lock of black hair falling across his forehead showed up at their meeting.

/ Their fate was sealed. The Nazi party would soon be born.

Adolf Hitler had never heard of the group the army sent him to observe, but he found that it espoused many of his ideas. He was startled when its members invited him to join. But there was something appealing about "this absurd little organization." It was an opportunity Hitler could not pass up. He hoped that "through just such a little movement the rise of the nation could some day be organized."[1] He hesitated briefly, then signed on as head of recruitment and propaganda.

The German Workers' party, up to that point, had been a sort of elitist debating club. Hitler quickly changed that by remaking it into a party that would appeal to the masses. Attendance at meetings grew, with Hitler's fiery speeches as the main draw. He would work himself into a frenzy and seem on the verge of losing all control, then would quiet down. He would denounce an imaginary plot by Socialists, Communists, Jews, and Allied powers to bring down Germany, but would always offer the hope of national unity and renewal. It wasn't so much that he *persuaded* listeners, but that he sensed their feelings and reflected their mood back at them, seeming to speak from their very hearts.

At a February 24, 1920, meeting of about two thousand people, Hitler got the party to change its name to the National Socialist German Workers' party—thereafter known as the Nazi party, a shortening of its German name. Where other German political parties aimed at specific groups or classes of people, Hitler presented the Nazi party with a twenty-five-point program with provisions to appeal to just about everyone. Much of it was ultimately ignored, but some points were followed precisely. Point twenty-five said: "For modern society, a colossus with feet of clay, we shall create an unprecedented centralization, which will unite all powers in the hands of the government. We shall create a hierarchical constitution, which will mechanically govern all movements of individuals."[2] In addition, the program promised to force Jews out of public life. These would become the guiding principles of the Nazi party.

⚲ Within two months, Hitler was off the army's payroll and working full time at political agitation. By the end of the year, supporters bought an anti-Semitic Munich newspaper called the *People's Observer*, which became the official party paper. A group of young Nazi roughnecks was organized into a paramilitary unit that would become the Sturmabteilung (SA), the party's "storm troopers," under Ernst Röhm. Hitler put down all who opposed him within the party and made himself, in essence, the party's dictator. He organized the party around his Fuehrerprinzip, or leadership principle, which called for strong leadership at all levels and obedience to authority.

BUILDING A FOLLOWING. By 1921, Hitler's meetings were drawing crowds in the thousands. Violence was already the party's trademark. Why was anyone interested in this party of right-wing extremists and bullies? The appeal of the Nazis has to be examined against the backdrop of the politics of the period in Weimar Germany.

The Weimar government was in trouble almost from the start because people associated the new leaders with the humiliating Treaty of Versailles. Right-wing nationalist parties called the treaty's signers the "November criminals," an image Hitler made much use of.

Strikes and demonstrations rattled industry in 1919 and 1920. Coups were attempted, one after another. Communists, with encouragement from Moscow, were staging occasional uprisings. Although the rebellions were easily put down, they created the impression that a Communist takeover could happen at any time.

Since no political party held a majority of seats in the German parliament, the Reichstag, parties had to form coalitions in order to amass enough votes to pass laws. The Reichstag coalition that approved the new constitution in 1919 fell apart with the election of June 1920, and from then on the assembly wobbled from one ruling coalition to the next. In the course of the decade, Germany was ruled by twenty coalition governments in rapid succession. It is no wonder the people had little faith in the ability of their parliamentary government to get anything done.

And along came Hitler, railing against the government, bemoaning its betrayal of the army, calling for a renewal of national pride and power, and, most sinister of all, offering up a scapegoat—the Jews. It was a powerful combination of ideas, offered to desperate people.

In 1921 the Nazi banner, with the black swastika on a white disk against a red background, was first flown at one of the mass meetings that doubled as party fund-raisers. Hitler was building a following in Munich, and he demanded loyalty and activism, knowing this would serve not to alienate people but rather to make them feel more bound to the Nazi party. He gave them symbols and rituals, just a taste of the spectacular rallies the party would stage in years to come. But the party, with its radical ideas, remained on the fringe of German politics.

What Hitler needed to push more people into his grasp was a national disaster. In 1923 it looked like he would get more than one. The French, claiming Germany had reneged on its World War I reparations, sent soldiers into Germany's coal-rich Ruhr region on January 11, 1923. The German military was in no condition to resist, so the people fought back by going on strike. The government led the campaign of passive resistance. Trains stopped running, mines were abandoned, machines were stilled. At first the strike seemed to be effective. But before long, it became clear the Germans were hurting themselves more than they were hurting the French.

The government printed huge amounts of money to pay idle Ruhr workers. This brought on an inflation that exploded into hyperinflation. Money became all but worthless. People carried paper money in boxes and wheelbarrows. Workers had to be paid three times a day, because the wages they received in the morning were not enough to buy lunch by noon. Banks printed more zeroes on existing bills to try to keep up with the dizzying crash of the German currency. Fortunes were wiped out. Life became chaotic. There was only one way out: On September 24, 1923, the German government called a halt to the so-called Ruhr war.

Most people in the middle class had lost everything they had. They blamed the government. Within the fires of national discontent, Adolf Hitler saw the flame of opportunity.

THE BEER HALL PUTSCH. Hitler decided to make a grab for power in the state of Bavaria, of which Munich was the capital, and enlisted the support of the popular General Erich Ludendorff. On the evening of November 8, 1923, the political leaders of

Bavaria were assembled in a Munich beer hall. Hitler had his SA men surround the building. Then he rushed in with pistol in hand, climbed onto a chair, and fired a shot at the ceiling. The hall was suddenly silent. Hitler strode to the platform and announced that the national revolution had begun and that the army and police were marching on the city under the Nazi banner. This last was pure bluff.

He led the three top Bavarian leaders to a side room, where he threatened and browbeat them. When the four returned to the hall, Hitler announced that they had made a pact to work together, and his captives made a show of shaking hands and agreeing. But it was only a show, and at the first opportunity they slipped out of Hitler's grasp.

The next day, at Ludendorff's insistence, Hitler and his followers tried to stage an armed march on the city. The planned show of Nazi power was a disaster. Police fired on them. In less than a minute, fourteen Nazis and three policemen had been fatally shot. Hitler was the first to flee, leaving his dead and injured comrades lying in the street. He didn't get far.

Hitler was charged with treason for what came to be known as the Beer Hall Putsch. He turned his trial into a propaganda triumph, taking advantage of the fact that newspapers all over Germany were playing the story on the front page. At last he had a national audience! He proclaimed that he was responsible for the rebellion and that it had been no crime, because the government leaders were the real traitors to the German people. In his closing speech, he said: "The man who is born to be a dictator is not compelled; he wills it. He is not driven forward, but drives himself."[3]

The court sentenced Hitler to five years; he served less than one, from April 1 to December 20,

Hitler's storm troopers arrest Marxist leaders in the Beer Hall Putsch. Hitler was sent to jail when his Nazi *putsch,* or revolution, failed. He succeeded, however, in reaching a national audience.

1924. While he was in prison, he began dictating *Mein Kampf* (*My Struggle*), a rambling, two-volume work that was part autobiography, part political statement. In *Mein Kampf*, Hitler laid out his plans for conquest, saying that Germans needed more living space, or Lebensraum, and should seize territory in the East. He expressed his contempt for parliamentary government and described the value of propaganda and of focusing people's anger on a single foe. He went on at length about a master "Aryan" race, supposedly made up of brilliant, honest, creative, and physically superior people. (There is no such thing as an Aryan race, and neither Hitler nor his top aides had the Nordic looks that Nazis considered characteristic of this "race.") In his book, Hitler repeatedly blamed Germany's troubles on Marxists and Jews. "Was there any form of filth or profligacy," he wrote, ". . . without at least one Jew involved in it?"4

When the first volume was published in 1925, *Mein Kampf* was regarded as the weird but harmless blatherings of a would-be revolutionary who had failed in his lunge for power. Even Hitler's associates considered it something of an embarrassment, not at all a fitting complement to his powerful speeches.

Hitler emerged from prison to find the party in disarray. He was prohibited from making public speeches, a ban that lasted almost three years in some parts of Germany. The party had also been banned and its newspaper suppressed. As Hitler tells it, he was by now firmly convinced of his mission and equally firm in his determination to take power not by force but by legal means.

POLITICAL DEFEAT, POLITICAL VICTORY. Hitler also found when he got out of prison that the country was getting back on its feet. The government had managed to stabilize the currency, and German industry was beginning to rebuild, modernize, and prosper again. National income was rising and unemployment was falling. French troops were leaving the Ruhr. Germany was admitted to the League of Nations in 1926. People began to gain faith in the government.

This was bad news for the Nazis, as well as for their left-wing political counterparts, the Communists. In general, both extremist parties saw their support among voters rise when times were bad. As a result of Germany's apparent recovery in the mid-twenties, both parties lost seats in the Reichstag.

Hitler was not ready to give up. He knew the disaster he longed for would occur, and with unshakable faith in that dark vision, he prepared to rescue Germany from it. He built an elaborate administrative machine, even though party membership was still too small to justify such an organization. The Nazis also assembled a nationwide grass-roots network of activists, reaching into every village and factory. Hitler decided that a coup would never work. Instead, Nazis should run for seats in the Reichstag in order to destroy the parliament from within. Ruffians of the SA kept up the street fighting with Communists.

Despite the party's organizing and endless rabble-rousing, it suffered a stunning defeat in elections of May 20, 1928, capturing only twelve seats out of six hundred in the Reichstag. But trouble for the nation—and opportunity for Hitler—loomed. The economy was beginning to stumble. Farmers had been suffering from a recession for several years. When the American stock market crashed in October 1929 and touched off a worldwide depression, the German economy came crashing down, too. Lenders called in loans, businesses went bankrupt, farmers were forced to sell their land. The memory of the hyperinflation of 1923 was fresh, and those who had jobs or wealth or status were keenly aware that these could all vanish in an instant.

Once again, Hitler was ready to exploit disaster. He sensed, as many politicians did not, that people did not want a detailed plan for turning the economy

By 1927, Hitler, a clever politician with an ability to organize, had turned the Nazis into an important minority party.

around. What Germans wanted was someone to lift their spirits and restore their sense of national pride. The Nazi party campaigned nonstop, even when no election was approaching, offering an array of appealing and often contradictory promises.

The government was scrambling to form a coalition in the Reichstag to try to pull Germany out of its economic quagmire. An election was set for September 14, 1930. This, Hitler thought, would be his chance to get more Nazis into the legislature. Nazi activists mounted a massive campaign, harping on the failures of the Weimar government and relentlessly attacking everything about the existing system. Nazis hoped to win as many as fifty seats in the Reichstag.

The election results shocked Nazi critics and supporters alike. The party polled 6.4 million votes and captured 107 seats in the Reichstag, making it the nation's second-strongest party.

Adolf Hitler was no longer on the fringe of German politics. The stunning election results gave his party the breakthrough he had sought for ten years. The temperamental Austrian demagogue was now a key player in the national arena.

OUT WITH THE OLD

Sooner will a camel pass through
a needle's eye than a great man
be "discovered" by an election.

In world history the man who
really rises above the norm
of the broad average usually
announces himself personally.

ADOLF HITLER
MEIN KAMPF

Hitler leaves the home of Paul von Hindenburg after a private talk in 1933. Despite his grave misgivings, the aging president buckled under pressure and named Hitler chancellor that year.

NOW THAT HE HAD demonstrated that the Nazi party commanded a massive following, Hitler still had to work his way into the centers of power. The sentries guarding the way would prove, in the end, incapable of stopping the cunning newcomer.

President Paul von Hindenburg, a popular hero of World War I, was in his eighties. As head of state, he had the power to hire or fire a chancellor, to dissolve the parliament and call new elections, and to rule by decree in an emergency. He found Hitler obnoxious and had no intention of letting him gain power in the German government. Heinrich Brüning, a former army captain and legislator, was chancellor, or head of the government. He had the army's backing when he was appointed in early 1930, and he hoped to bring back stable, democratic government. General Wilhelm Groener, defense minister, had tried without success to cleanse the army of Nazi influence.

Without knowing it, Brüning set the stage for German acceptance of Hitler's Reich. Since March 1930, at Brüning's suggestion, Germany had been governed under the emergency powers granted in Article 48 of the Weimar constitution. This meant government by decree; once Hindenburg had invoked Article 48, he and his cabinet could make laws without having to get a majority of parliament to vote for the laws. Brüning used emergency decrees to force unpopular economic measures on the public, such as lower wages and pensions and higher taxes. The moves did not repair the crumbling economy, but they did infuriate German voters.

Hitler kept up his attacks on the government in speeches and in the party newspaper, meanwhile taking care to assure the army that the Nazi party would be its salvation. Nazis in the Reichstag used that institution as a forum to berate the government. The last thing on their minds was to actually participate in parliamentary government.

The Nazi message seemed to strike a chord with the public. Party membership grew by 100,000 between the September election and the end of 1930. Then the catastrophe Hitler longed for arrived: Unemployment soared to more than 6 million in 1931. Austria's largest bank collapsed, and German banks followed. Homeless people set up tent villages around major cities. Farmers posted armed guards on their land, but hungry people raided the fields anyway.

During that year, Hitler began to cultivate the support of business leaders. And he continued wooing the army, which remained eager to rearm and to see the Weimar democracy collapse. Through it all, he stuck with his plan to use only legal tactics.

Hitler had two psychological weapons in his arsenal. First, the SA was agitating for a chance to step up the violence, and the government saw Hitler as the person who could keep the SA menace in check. And second, since he could muster so much voter support, Hitler was perceived as a useful political ally. By the time the Weimar leaders figured out that Hitler wasn't going to let himself be used by anyone, it was too late.

PERSONAL AND POLITICAL SETBACKS. In these years of increasing political power, Hitler had what appears to have been the one great love of his life. His half-sister, Angela Raubal, and her two daughters had moved in with Hitler in the late 1920s, and Hitler fell in love with his pretty niece Geli. By 1931 the relationship had soured, and Geli made plans to leave Hitler's Munich home and move to Vienna. In a loud and public exchange, Hitler forbade it. The next morning, September 18, twenty-three-year-old Geli was found dead from a gunshot wound. Her death was ruled a suicide.

Hitler was devastated. He went into seclusion and for weeks had trouble eating, sleeping, and working. Associates, fearing he would try to kill himself, took away his revolver and watched him constantly. Hitler created his own one-person cult around Geli, a devotion that would last the rest of his life. He ordered that her room in Munich be kept exactly as she had left it, and a painting and a sculpture of her would later hold places of honor in his other homes. Throughout his life, he would carry her picture along with his mother's. Historians believe the shock of Geli's death prompted him to forgo eating most meat from then on.

Before long, Hitler recovered enough to turn his attention back to his political ambitions. The aging German president, Hindenburg, was scheduled to retire in the spring of 1932, but aides talked him into running again. Hitler decided to gamble his new political prestige and challenge Hindenburg. Still an Austrian citizen at this point, Hitler hurriedly had a Nazi official in the state of Brunswick grant him German citizenship so he could run for office. The Nazi propaganda staff, led by Joseph Goebbels, launched a media blitz. In the space of a few weeks, thousands of rallies and parades were staged. Whenever Hitler was to speak, busloads of supporters were brought in. The venue would always be too small, giving the impression that Hitler drew standing-room-only crowds. Nazis sold autographed copies of *Mein Kampf* and other souvenirs at Hitler's campaign stops. The idea was to nurture the image of Adolf Hitler, superstar.

Hitler failed to win a majority in the March 13 election and had to battle Hindenburg again in a runoff on April 10. Hitler lost that election, too. Nonetheless, the campaign made him Hindenburg's peer in the eyes of the public.

The winter of 1931–1932 had seen escalating violence between Nazis and Communists, and in April the government banned the SA. For months, Hitler and a few scheming leaders in the government cooked up plots and counterplots. The chancellorship changed hands twice in 1932. Germany was sinking into political chaos. Amid this turmoil, Hitler manipulated Hindenburg into dissolving the Reichstag and setting elections for July 31, 1932. It would be the third national election that year. The Nazis, hoping to gain more Reichstag seats, put on the most massive, sophisticated campaign that Germans had ever seen. The party seemed to be on the threshold of power. When the votes were counted, the Nazis had captured 38 percent, making the party for the first time the strongest in Germany. But it had still fallen short of the majority the Nazis had expected.

In fact, although no one knew it at the time, the July 1932 vote was the best showing the Nazis would make in a free election. When Germans faced yet another national election in November 1932, the Nazis won only 33 percent. Party leaders were mortified. Their slew of contradictory promises (telling farmers they would get more money for their produce, for instance, while telling city dwellers they would see lower food prices) were catching up with them. The majority of people who voted for the Nazis, it turned out, were really just voting in protest against the Weimar system.

But now personality came into play. Franz von Papen, a favorite of President Hindenburg who had had a fleeting tenure as chancellor in 1932, schemed with Hitler to recapture the office together. Hitler agreed to team up with Papen if Papen would accept the vice chancellorship and back Hitler as chancellor. In addition, Hitler got Papen to agree that a few other offices would be given to Nazis.

On January 30, 1933, the weary Hindenburg gave in to their pressure and appointed Hitler chancellor. Aides assured him that the irritating former corporal could be kept under control. In little more than the blink of an eye, they saw how wrong they had been.

THE NAZIS TAKE OVER. The posts Hitler demanded for Nazis were crucial ones. Hermann Göring was made deputy commissar for Prussia, giving him control of the police in Germany's largest state. And Wilhelm Frick became interior minister, in charge of police throughout the rest of Germany. Now that their leader was truly in power, the SA went wild, beating and killing Communists, Jews, priests, journalists, and whomever else they chose—without interference from the police. Communists threatened to lead a work stoppage. In the uproar, Hitler got Hindenburg to sign a decree allowing the government to suppress newspapers and ban public meetings. Elected officials were purged, and Nazi supporters were installed in their place. Göring declared that the Prussian police needed help, so Nazi storm troopers were sworn in as arms of the law.

Then, on the night of February 27, the Reichstag building in Berlin was torched. A young Dutch former Communist, Marinus van der Lubbe, was caught starting the fire. The Nazis immediately blamed their archenemies and began to arrest Communists by the thousands. They also drafted what came to be known as the Reichstag fire decree, which suspended freedom of the press, privacy in mail and telephone communications, and other civil rights. The decree gave the Nazis the legal authority to arrest and imprison people without trials.

Jails quickly overflowed, and the SA had to find some way to "concentrate" these prisoners. It used abandoned warehouses and gymnasiums and then, with no direction from the government, began setting up concentration camps as places to get opponents out of circulation and beat them up.

Less than a month after Hitler had come into power, the Reichstag (parliament) building was set on fire. The Nazis fingered their favorite scapegoat, Communists, as the arsonists, and under the pretext of protecting the country suspended civil and human rights.

Making the most of the Reichstag fire, the Nazi propaganda machine kicked into overdrive in an effort to whip up fear of a Communist menace before the next election, which was scheduled for March 5, 1933. But the combination of promotion and intimidation was still not enough. In an election that could hardly be called free, the Nazis polled only 43.9 percent, still short of the majority that Hitler had always wanted.

It didn't matter. Hitler called it a victory anyway, and Nazi terror reached new extremes. Opponents of the Nazis in the Reichstag went into hiding or were arrested. Nazis took charge of all state governments.

Finally, on March 23, 1933, the Reichstag handed Hitler the power he sought. With its passage of a law called the Enabling Act, the German parliament gave all power to make and enforce laws to the chancellor and the cabinet. President Hindenburg, the widely revered World War I hero, remained as a figurehead.

With that—and without ever having won a majority of votes—Adolf Hitler legally became the dictator of Germany.

THE THOUSAND-YEAR REICH

**National Socialist Germany
wants peace because of
its fundamental convictions.**

**The principal effect of every
war is to destroy the flower of
the nation. Germany needs
peace and desires peace.**

ADOLF HITLER
MAY 21, 1935

A book burning in the early days of the
Third Reich. Schools were coerced into pro-
moting Nazi racist beliefs, histories were
rewritten, and the people, works of art, and
books that did not conform were destroyed.

NEW SPIRIT HAD infused Berlin. After more than a decade of misery and uncertainty, hope was in the air. If the new chancellor was rather extreme in some of his views, well, that could be overlooked. Germany was about to come alive again.

Such was the mood in the capital when Hitler took over as head of the German government. But he still had work to do to tighten his grip on the nation. He started at once.

First, opposition had to be put down. All political parties other than the Nazis were dissolved. Criticizing the government could land a person in prison. Judges were intimidated. Labor unions were smashed. The Vatican arranged a deal with Hitler:

Catholic schools could continue to exist, but church officials and organizations must refrain from political activity.

Hitler had more than the regular police to enforce his will. What began as an elite bodyguard in 1925 had evolved by 1933 into a powerful security force called the Schutzstaffel (protection squad), or SS. An arm of Göring's Prussian police grew into an organization whose name sent shivers of terror down many spines: the Geheime Staatspolizei (secret state police), or Gestapo. The two were merged in 1934 under the ruthless SS chief Heinrich Himmler, giving him control of all German police.

With coaxing as well as coercion, the Nazis pressed for conformity. State-sponsored Nazi organizations were set up for lawyers, teachers, farmers, athletes, artists, young people, women, professionals, and others. This gave people a sense of belonging and at the same time isolated them so as to shut down the free exchange of ideas. Schools were nazified, and courses from history to science to language were rewritten to reflect Nazi racist views. Hitler made a concentrated and largely successful effort to win over the young. The Hitler Youth became the only legal youth organization, and children from ages ten to eighteen were expected to join.

Hitler next began to remove Jews from German society in a way that wouldn't outrage the non-Jewish population. In an April 7, 1933, decree, government workers of "non-Aryan descent" were forced to retire. That same month, limits were placed on the number of "non-Aryans" who could attend schools and colleges. Laws explicitly aimed at Jews would come later. For a time, defining who was a Jew was a troublesome problem. What about Jews married to non-Jews, or the children of those marriages? What about people who had only one Jewish grandparent? Or people with Jewish parents who did not practice the Jewish religion? Did it matter whether a person considered himself or herself Jewish? Over the years, Nazi bureaucrats would develop a complex set of rules to deal with these questions.

With Hitler's control over Germany growing, the Law for Reconstruction of the Reich, on January 30, 1934, officially moved what power the states still held into the hands of the central government. Hitler was given authority to change the constitution at will.

The SA was still as rowdy as ever. But now that Hitler wanted to be seen as a dignified statesman, the group that had been so instrumental in his rise was an embarrassment. Hitler had made allies of the army, business leaders, and conservatives in the government, all of whom saw the SA as a threat. Hitler's solution involved deception and murder. With the help of the Gestapo, Hitler's henchmen cooked up phony evidence to frame Ernst Röhm, leader of the SA. The trap was set. On June 30, 1934, Hitler himself burst in on SA leaders who were expecting to meet with him later that day. He had them all arrested, and SS squads began executing them at once. The next night, Hitler had his longtime associate Röhm shot, too. Once the killing began, Hitler had other foes from the past murdered as well. The spree became known as the Blood Purge.

How could Hitler claim this bloodbath was legal? He had a law passed less than a week later making it legal *retroactively* and calling it necessary for national security. In effect, the SA purge was Hitler's bow to the army, which he wanted on his side. President Hindenburg also supported Hitler's action. After the purge, the SA continued to exist as a party organization, but it never regained its old clout. The SS took over control of the concentration camps.

In the summer of 1934, Hindenburg died, leaving Hitler at last free to rule without hindrance from the cranky old man. Although Hitler, as chancellor, was the head of the German government, the president had remained in his role as head of state. With Hindenburg's death, Hitler combined the two jobs. He jettisoned the title of president and declared himself Führer, or leader, of the German Reich and People. Now came his payback for the SA purge: The army swore an oath of loyalty not to the state but to Hitler personally. Hitler called his state the Third Reich. The First Reich, he said, had been the Holy Roman Empire of 962 to 1806; the Second had been created by Otto von Bismarck and lasted from 1871 to 1918. He predicted that his Reich, or empire, would last a thousand years.

STRENGTH THROUGH FEAR. Now that political threats had been put down, Hitler in 1935 stepped up his campaign against the Jews. A group of laws known as the Nuremberg Laws further isolated Jews from their non-Jewish friends, neighbors, and associates. The decrees prohibited Jews from marrying or having sex with non-Jews, employing non-Jewish German women of childbearing age in their households, or displaying the German flag. Jews were stripped of their German citizenship and were declared "subjects." Bit by bit, in ways that came to be accepted by the public, and always under the guise of legality, Jews were pushed toward their doom.

Although Hitler's drive to wipe out Jews is what history remembers most about him, the process did not draw as much attention while it was happening as it has in retrospect. Anti-Semitism had always been central to the Nazi program, and the Nazis never tried to hide their rabid hatred of Jews. But in the early years, German people saw it as just one more issue among many Nazi issues. They did not foresee that this would be the one idea on which the Nazis would never weaken their position. What people did notice was that they could get jobs again. In 1933, with 6 million people out of work, Germany had the worst unemployment in Europe. Three years later, thanks to Hitler's push to rearm and his public works projects, there were more jobs available than people to fill them.

Hitler was also casting off the chains of the hated Versailles Treaty. His predecessors had started this. Secret plans to rearm had been in the works since the mid-twenties, and Germany's reparation payments had been brought to an end in 1932. Hitler ordered that the army be tripled in size (to 300,000) and told Göring to secretly build an air force. He made eloquent speeches about peace but pulled Germany out of an international disarmament conference and the League of Nations.

A system of alliances had developed among European nations to preserve peace and, in effect, to keep Germany from starting another war. Hitler took aim at this arrangement by making a ten-year non-aggression pact with Poland, announced on January 26, 1934. As the Poles would learn, the pact was a scam. But it served to drive a wedge between the Poles and their allies, the French. In March 1935, Hitler revealed the existence of the German Air

By 1936, when this photo was taken, Hitler was in brazen violation of the Treaty of Versailles, which forbade Germany to rearm after its defeat in World War I. Europe did nothing to stop him.

Force, revived the draft, and announced that the German Army would be expanded to half a million. The British and the French protested, but they did nothing to stop him. Hitler then concluded a naval agreement with the British that allowed Germany to rapidly rebuild its navy. The pact infuriated the French. The anti-German alliances were unraveling.

Seeing what Hitler accomplished in just a few years, Germans were dazzled. There was no more violence in the streets. Their economy was booming. Germany was flexing its military muscles before the nations that had humiliated it. Hitler seemed a miracle worker. Wherever he went in the early years of his rule, cheering crowds gathered to toss flowers at his car or demand autographs.

But there was also a darker side to life under Hitler. The Nazis kept life orderly by being everywhere. Virtually everyone was expected to join one Nazi organization or another. Nazi rallies and celebrations occurred almost weekly—on Hitler's birthday, the Beer Hall Putsch anniversary, a memorial day for a Nazi martyr, and on and on. Children were fed Nazi doctrine in school, then more of it in the Hitler Youth. They were encouraged to report any anti-Hitler remarks made by their parents. Each neighborhood had a Nazi block captain to make sure everyone listened to Hitler's speeches on the radio and put out the flag on his birthday. Nazi informants spied on people in shops, on the street, even in church.

Gestapo arrests were made at night to inspire fear and uncertainty. Gestapo agents strung prisoners up by their hands, which were tied behind their backs. They slashed prisoners' feet with razors and forced them to walk on salt. They stuck pins in the eyes of captives, commanded police dogs to tear prisoners apart, or tortured prisoners with electric shocks. You never knew when a casual wisecrack would land you in a Gestapo office or a concentration camp. Could you share your thoughts with your neighbor? Would he join you if you protested? Was it worth the risk? Or wouldn't it be better, safer, just to keep quiet and mind your own business?

This was what the Nazis counted on: People would be too apathetic, or too worried about saving their own skins, to band together and fight back. This everyday terror was the price Germans paid for the order Hitler brought to their lives.

Hitler, basking in the glow of his power, planned grand monuments to himself. He ordered his architect, Albert Speer, to design a huge complex in Nuremberg for the annual Nazi party rallies. He wanted Berlin rebuilt into a city whose magnificence would put Paris and Vienna to shame. These were plans he had toyed with in the mid-twenties, when he was being written off as a political failure. Hitler still thought of himself as an artist, and architecture fascinated him. He loved to look at building plans and could quickly memorize drawings in detail. He always treated architects with respect. Others around him did not fare as well.

THE INNER CIRCLE. Eva Braun, Hitler's lover, had to endure loneliness and humiliation to be with him. Hitler and Braun had met in October 1929 while she was working for his photographer, Heinrich Hoffmann. They became lovers in early 1932, a few months after Geli Raubal's death. Toward the end of that year, desperate to get Hitler to pay more attention to her, Braun had tried to commit suicide by shooting herself. Although she became Hitler's only permanent mistress, Braun never seemed to capture his heart the way his niece had. Her diary from 1935 records the emotional roller coaster he kept her on. In February she wrote: "I am so infinitely happy that he loves me so much, and I pray that it will always be like this. . . . I am so terribly unhappy that I cannot write to him."[1]

When anyone of importance visited his mountain home, the Berghof, Braun had to stay upstairs, out of sight. She could sometimes sit next to Hitler at large dinners, but he did not permit her to speak to him. In May 1935 she brooded in her diary: "The weather is so

Eva Braun shares a relaxed moment with Adolf Hitler and their dogs. Although she was his mistress for more than fifteen years, she had no influence on his political life, nor did she ever seek the spotlight.

wonderful and I, the mistress of the greatest man in Germany and in the world, am sitting here and gazing at the sun through a window."[2] Later that month, she tried again to kill herself, this time with sleeping pills. Hitler's callous disregard for her feelings often left her in despair. He sometimes remarked in her presence that he would never want to be around a witty or intelligent woman. But despite his neglect and disrespectfulness, she stuck by him.

As for the men who served him with such loyalty, Hitler often ridiculed them behind their backs, and they mirrored his malice in their dealings with each other. His highest aides feuded constantly, scheming to snatch turf from each other and to undermine each other's standing with the Führer. Amid the endless squabbling, bureaucratic chaos became a hallmark of Hitler's regime. Hitler seemed to encourage this, giving vague orders or assigning the same task to several people at the same time and then letting underlings fight over who was responsible for what. Many scrambled to build their own fiefdoms: The Gestapo and the SS, in fact, grew out of the unchecked empire-building of Göring and Himmler. Hitler, the master manipulator of crowds, was forever being manipulated by the men closest to him, particularly conniving Goebbels, arrogant Göring, and ambitious Himmler.

They were a crew well suited to the topsy-turvy world of the Nazi Reich. Himmler especially took Hitler's racist views to heart and developed bizarre pseudo-religious beliefs in a mystical Germanic race. He wanted his SS to be a group of racially elite aristocrats, and he required recruits to prove their racial "purity" going back several generations. Göring, the head of the air force (the Luftwaffe), was a morphine addict who loved gourmet food and other trappings of wealth. Over the years he amassed a collection of artworks, jewelry, and fine liqueurs from the spoils of Nazi looting. He polished his fingernails, rouged his cheeks, and dressed in velvet robes. Goebbels, minister of popular enlightenment and propaganda, was a

From left to right: Hermann Göring, Hitler's second in command; Adolf Hitler; Joseph Goebbels, chief Nazi propagandist; and SS leader Heinrich Himmler.

master at cutting down his rivals in Hitler's view. His ministry controlled news media, literature, music, radio, movies, theater, and the fine arts. He was a talented orator, second only to Hitler in his ability to stir up crowds.

Hitler had his own idiosyncrasies. He fretted often about his health, complained about stomach pains, and feared that he would die soon. He resisted efforts by his aides to get him to see a first-rate doctor. Instead, he fell under the spell of the little-respected Dr. Theodor Morell, who told Hitler that his ailments were caused by stress and began injecting him with drugs, vitamins, and other substances. Hitler tried to control his weight with laxatives and enemas. He stayed up well past midnight every night, watching movies and talking endlessly while guests feigned interest, and he rarely began work before noon.

These were the key men in Germany's ruling clique in the 1930s—a cabal of unpleasant personalities with their hands full of power. As the decade wore on, they used that power to drive the nation inexorably toward war and mass murder.

A program called the Four-Year Plan was established in 1936 to prepare the economy for war and to make Germany self-sufficient and therefore invulnerable to a wartime blockade. Göring, who knew little about economics, was put in charge of it. The Four-Year Plan told businesses what to make, where to make it, and how to spend their profits. The police and SS were merged under Himmler's command the same year. Meanwhile, the army made the transition from preparing to defend Germany to preparing to attack.

The pieces were falling into place. It was time for Hitler to start making his moves.

BLOODLESS CONQUEST

5

What we must fight for is to
safeguard the existence and
reproduction of our race and
our people, so that our people
may mature for the fulfillment
of the mission allotted it by
the creator of the universe.

ADOLF HITLER
MEIN KAMPF

Adolf Hitler with Benito Mussolini after forming the Rome-Berlin Axis in 1937. Like Hitler, Mussolini had pushed his way into absolute power, as dictator of Italy. His Fascist regime controlled industry, the media, and education.

HITLER TALKED A good game about conquest and "living space," or Lebensraum. But would other nations let him get away with his plans?

Expansion of Germany had begun quietly and without conflict in January 1935. That month, residents of the Saarland, a coal-rich area on the French-German border, voted on whether their region should rejoin Germany, join France, or remain under League of Nations administration as it had been since the war. The residents voted by a 90 percent margin to become part of Germany. Hitler declared another fetter of the Treaty of Versailles broken.

He then made a move that he later called the most daring of his career. Germany's industrial Rhineland area, also along the French border, had been demilitarized under the Treaty of Versailles. Sending German troops there would be a slap in the face of the Allies, especially France. On March 7, 1936, Hitler did just that. Had the French resisted, Hitler later admitted, the German troops would have had to flee in humiliation. The French issued a protest, along with the British, but they did not fight. Instead, the Allied powers clung to the belief that war could be avoided if only they could appease Hitler.

Meanwhile, civil war broke out in Spain in July 1936. Hitler and Italian dictator Benito Mussolini jumped in to support the rebellion of Francisco Franco. Here was the perfect combat training ground for German officers and pilots and a chance to test the weapons and planes Germany was building. The last thing Hitler wanted was to help end the Spanish Civil War. Rather, he wanted to drag out the fighting to draw attention away from Germany's rush to rearm.

In 1936–1937, Hitler was developing his own system of alliances in anticipation of war. With Mussolini he formed a pact hostile to the British and the Communists. That alliance, the Rome-Berlin Axis, was formalized in September 1937. Germany and Japan signed an agreement of anti-Communist cooperation, called the Anti-Comintern Pact, on November 25, 1936. Secret clauses provided that neither would help the Soviet Union if it attacked the other. Italy joined the pact in November 1937.

Hitler made no secret of his intentions among his military chiefs. In a meeting on November 5, 1937, he told them that the German racial community of 85 million needed more living space, and that he planned to get it by 1945—by force. Austria and Czechoslovakia, Germany's neighbors to the south and southeast, would have to be conquered so they could not threaten Germany and so they could supply food for Germans. The British and the French might fight the Germans over these moves, but that was a risk Hitler was willing to take.

When two generals spoke up against this lunacy, Himmler and Göring cooked up scandals about them, involving prostitution, lewd photographs, and homosexuality. Within three months, the dissenters were out of their jobs. Furthermore, Hitler took over as head of the army and kicked out sixty other troublesome generals, as well as some government officials he considered unreliable.

Now Hitler was free to take another gamble—making Austria part of his greater German Reich. This was not a new idea. Many Austrians, especially Austrian Nazis, wanted union with Germany. The Allies opposed such a union, but would they fight to stop it? Hitler was ready to bet they would not.

Austrian Chancellor Kurt von Schuschnigg could see what was brewing and went to the Berghof in early 1938 to offer Hitler a deal. Schuschnigg hoped to fend off German incursions by offering Austrian Nazis a share of power. Hitler flew into a rage—a carefully staged one. He demanded more concessions and threatened to send in troops within days. Intimidated, Schuschnigg waffled for several weeks and finally resigned in the face of the Nazi threat.

ANSCHLUSS. On the morning of March 12, 1938, after Mussolini had agreed not to interfere, German troops streamed into Austria. That afternoon, Hitler himself went to his native land. Cheering crowds greeted him everywhere. The Führer was touched. The next day, the Anschluss, or annexation, was proclaimed: "Austria is a province of the German Reich."[1] Arrests began that night. About 40,000 police and SS men followed the army into Austria and went after Austria's 300,000 Jews as well as potential opponents of the Nazis. Despite the violence, people on both sides of the border were enthusiastic about the annexation, and Hitler's popularity in Germany soared.

British Prime Minister Neville Chamberlain accepted the Anschluss, declaring that it would not have been worth a war to try to stop it. The French, likewise, did nothing to interfere with Hitler's move. The gamble had paid off. The Allies were not willing to fight.

Anyone who looked at a map of Europe could see what the Anschluss meant to Czechoslovakia; the nation now had German forces across its borders on three sides. The fears of Czechoslovakia would soon be justified. In Hitler's plan to destroy the Czechoslovakian state, several factors came into play. The democratic nation had been created by the World War I peace settlements that Hitler despised. Much of its population belonged to an ethnic group called Slavs; Hitler had long ago decided that Slavic people were subhumans. But those people he held in such contempt had built a formidable system of frontier defenses and an arms industry that Hitler wanted to put to work for Germany. In addition, there were more than 3 million people of German descent, known as ethnic Germans, living in the Sudeten region of Czechoslovakia. This German minority gave Hitler the excuse he sought.

Within weeks of the Anschluss, the Czech crisis, which would drag on for a year, began. Hitler sent instructions to Nazi supporters in the Sudetenland to

Hitler is greeted by children in Vienna. Germany annexed Austria without firing a shot, but the SS began its surreptitious attack on Jews and political opponents that very night.

present impossible demands to the Czech government. Meanwhile, Hitler threw up a smoke screen, raving that Sudeten Germans were suffering miserable treatment. In May 1938, he told his military leaders that he would smash Czechoslovakia by October 1.

The British and the French, anxious to avoid war, tried to calm Hitler by pressuring Czechoslovakia to meet the Germans' demands. German civilians, too, wanted to avoid war. So did the generals and the soldiers. In September, Czech president Edvard Beneš offered to concede everything the Germans wanted. But Hitler stepped up his demands. Now he wanted Czechoslovakia to let the Sudeten Germans decide for themselves whether to make their region part of Germany.

Once again the British and the French pressured Czechoslovakia, and the Czechs agreed. But when Chamberlain brought the news to Hitler on September 22, the Führer declared that it was too late; he was going to send troops in anyway. After a flurry of sword-rattling on all sides, Hitler agreed to meet with the leaders of Britain, France, and Italy to work out an agreement. The victim, Czechoslovakia, was not invited.

What came of the conference in Munich on September 29, 1938, was the disgraceful Munich Agreement in which 11,000 square miles (28,490 square kilometers) of Czechoslovakia were handed to Hitler. And German troops marched in on October 1 after all. Within the course of six months, what was left of Czechoslovakia was further carved up. Part of it was swept into Germany's Lebensraum, marking Hitler's first move into territory where the population was not primarily German; part went to Hungary (which had joined the Axis), and part was left as the puppet state of Slovakia. By mid-March 1939, the nation of Czechoslovakia had ceased to exist. Its demise was followed by the protests Hitler had come to expect from the British and the French.

KRISTALLNACHT. Another event in Germany shook the world in the autumn of 1938. The Gestapo had rounded up tens of thousands of Jews of Polish descent and dumped them across the Polish border. A distraught Jewish teenager, whose father had been among the deportees, shot a German diplomat to death in Paris on November 7. With prompting from a speech by Goebbels, the SA burst into action on the night of November 9 in the first nationally coordinated violent attack on Jews.

They burned synagogues, wrecked and looted Jewish-owned businesses, and murdered dozens of Jews while the police stood by. The SS arrested thousands of Jews and hauled them off to concentration camps. The burst of terror became known as Kristallnacht, the Night of Broken Glass, because of all the windows left in shards in the streets. As if the violence itself wasn't enough, Jews were forced to pay the costs of cleaning up the rubble.

Most Germans were appalled at the state-sponsored violence of Kristallnacht. In light of the public outrage, the regime decided that the so-called Jewish problem could not be solved by street thugs. The matter would have to be handled more quietly. Jews would have to be pushed out of German economic life and then driven out of Germany. The expulsion (and eventually the extermination) of the

Kristallnacht (the Night of Broken Glass),
a vicious state-sponsored attack against Jews,
caused enough outrage among Germans
that the Nazis resorted to more covert
methods of extermination in the future.

Jews fell into the hands of bureaucrats. It was a turning point in Nazi policy. On New Year's Day 1939, a
Central Office for Jewish Emigration was established.
About 430,000 Jews from Germany and Austria were
gotten rid of by emigration. They were the lucky ones.

A practice developed at about the same time that
would have far-reaching consequences for the Jews.

Nazi doctors quietly began the "mercy killing" of physically and mentally handicapped children in institutions. Some were overdosed with sedatives, others were slowly starved. Eventually, adult mental patients were also "euthanized." The method of killing: poison gas. It was just a preview of the horrors that later years would hold.

For the time being, Hitler seemed to be getting his way on all fronts. Jews were feeling the sting of his wrath. Leaders of other nations were letting him seize territory, not with guns but with threats. The German arms industry was building a war machine. Hitler made one more territorial demand in March 1939. He bullied Lithuania into handing over the port district of Memel, which Germany had lost after the Treaty of Versailles. This would be his last bloodless conquest.

Once Hitler dismantled Czechoslovakia, it didn't take a psychic to see that Poland was next on his hit list. The British and the French announced in March 1939 that if Hitler attacked Poland, they would help Poland fight back. Hitler was not deterred. He ordered the military to prepare to make a swift, massive attack on Poland by September 1, 1939.

A nervous world girded for war. Göring and Goebbels urged peace, to no avail. Hitler had been trying to forge a military alliance among Germany, Italy, and Japan, but the Japanese refused to sign. Germany and Italy finally made their own Pact of Steel on May 22, agreeing to join each other in war. That summer, Moscow was the partner with whom everyone wanted to dance. The British and the French courted Soviet dictator Joseph Stalin, hoping he could help them protect Poland.

But Hitler managed to sign up the Communist leader as an ally, with the fateful Nazi-Soviet Pact of August 23, 1939. The pact had a secret section that outlined the division of Poland between the Germans and the Soviets. Stalin saw in the pact a chance to gain control of eastern Europe without having to fight. Hitler still hated communism as much as ever, but he was a pragmatist. He didn't want the Soviets to intervene on the side of the Poles. The pact removed that threat.

Now the carnage of battle could begin.

WAR

Nature as such has not reserved
this soil for the future possession
of any particular nation or race;
on the contrary, this soil exists
for the people which possesses
the force to take it.

ADOLF HITLER
MEIN KAMPF

North Sea

GREAT BRITAIN

London

NETH.

BELGIUM

Paris

OCCUPIED FRANCE

VICHY FRANCE

Corsica

Sardinia

ALGERIA

TUNISIA

Mediterranean Sea

NORWAY

Oslo

SWEDEN

DENMARK

E. PRUSSIA

Bergen-Belsen

Berlin

GERMANY

Nuremberg

Dachau

Vienna

AUS.

ITALY

Sicily

FINLAND

Leningrad

Moscow

ESTONIA

LATVIA

RUSSIA

LITHUANIA

Stutthof

Culmhof

Chelmna

Auschwitz-Birkenau

Treblinka

Warsaw

POLAND

Sobibor

Lublin- Maidanek

Belzec

Plaszow

CZECH

HUN.

YUGO.

ROMANIA

Black Sea

BUL.

ALB.

GREECE

TURKEY

Crete

LIBYA

EGYPT

Prewar Germany

Areas controlled by Nazi Germany or its allies in 1942

■ Death Camps

▲ Concentration Camps

0   300 Miles

0   450 Kilometers

HITLER'S PLAN FOR
a new order in Europe had three basic elements: ridding Germany of people he considered racially undesirable, seizing more living space for his master race, and fighting communism. To Hitler these ideas were inseparable. He planned to annex territory in the East, kick out most of the Slavic people living there, and colonize it with ethnic Germans. Those Slavs who remained in German-controlled territory would be kept as an uneducated pool of slaves to serve the master race. Jews and Communists would be gotten rid of.

His strategy for waging war went something like this. He would take on one enemy at a time, first manipulating relationships among countries so that his target would be without allies. He would strike suddenly and massively, overwhelming his victim before any counterattack could be pulled together. The strategy was called Blitzkrieg, or lightning war. And for a time, it worked.

German troops barreled into Poland at dawn on September 1, 1939, while German warplanes roared overhead. Hitler was certain the British and the French would again back down. In a way, he was right; neither sent troops to fight. But both declared war on Germany on September 3. Hitler was stunned. He didn't want to go to war in the West just yet.

Nonetheless, the Germans rolled over the Poles within three weeks. From the east, Stalin's Red Army invaded Poland and took control of the nation's eastern half. By the end of the month, the Polish government had fled. The country was divided into three parts: Germany annexed the western third of Poland; Stalin held the eastern portion; and in between was a German-occupied territory that became known as the General Government.

So began World War II. Hitler boasted before the Reichstag on October 6 about his triumphs and vowed that he had no intention of making war with Britain or France. Less than two weeks later, he issued an order for an attack on the West. He declared Britain to be Germany's number-one enemy, but he never gave up his hope for an alliance with Britain.

CONTRADICTIONS. Hitler's attitude toward Britain was typical of the contradictions in his thinking and his policies. He expressed similar mixed feelings about religion, sometimes making harsh remarks about the church and other times declaring it an indispensable political tool. He still belonged to the Catho-

On September 1, 1939, Adolf Hitler announced that the "first shot had been fired by regular Polish soldiers," and that he had decided to send German divisions into Poland as a consequence. With these words, World War II began.

lic Church, as he would until his death. On the matter of sports, Hitler spoke often and with enthusiasm about the benefits of exercise, and he required German youngsters to take part in vigorous athletic activities. But he did not engage in sports himself.

Part of the reason he shunned sports was his self-conscious reluctance to do anything that might make him look silly. When Hitler got a new suit, he would have himself photographed in it so he could see how it looked before he wore it in public. If anyone walked up while he was playing with one of his dogs, he would hastily chase the dog away.

Now that his long-planned war was launched, Hitler at times seemed unable to grasp the seriousness of what he had started. He refused to listen to any real information about his opponents, relying instead upon his own instincts. He remained obsessed with his many building projects and ordered work on them to continue, despite the fact that construction experts, workers, and materials were needed at the battlefront to rebuild bridges and widen roads.

The conquest of Poland meant that Hitler could start experimenting with his theories about building a racially pure empire. He put Himmler in charge of moving people of Slavic heritage out and replacing them with people of German descent from other German-controlled territory. Polish children who fit the "Aryan" ideal that Hitler cherished—blond hair, blue eyes, strong bodies—were taken from their families and placed into special homes to be raised as Germans.

While Hitler lived in his world of glory and victory, however, his people sank into despair. No flowers were tossed at soldiers marching off to war, as they had been at the start of World War I. When

Hitler's motorcade rolled through Munich or Berlin, it was greeted only with silence. If he wanted a cheering crowd, his aides had to go out and organize one. The man who for years had drawn his strength from crowds now pulled away from a sullen public.

THE WESTERN OFFENSIVE. The Nazis and the Soviets, still in theory bound by their pact, were cooperating in several areas, including police work and trade. But Hitler was keeping an eye on Stalin and was drawing conclusions that would prove Hitler's undoing. For one thing, when the Germans and Russians met during the carving up of Poland, German troops found that their Soviet counterparts had wretched equipment. Then, in a brief war to take over Finland (November 1939 to March 1940), the Soviets suffered far heavier losses than the Finns. Clearly, Hitler thought, the Soviet Army was weak, badly organized, and no match for his racially superior German troops.

But it was not time to take on Stalin yet. On April 9, 1940, German diplomats in Denmark and Norway demanded that those nations accept German "protection" against the British and the French. The Danes capitulated, but the Norwegians resisted. Over the objections of his generals, Hitler launched an attack on Norway that morning. He surprised the Allies by invading from the sea and taking the main ports on Norway's long coast, while German airborne troops captured Norwegian airfields. Both were bold, unorthodox, and successful moves. By the end of June, Norway, too, was under Hitler's command.

One more thing had to be done before Hitler could invade the Soviet Union—the threat of attack in the West had to be squashed so that German forces could concentrate all their energy in the East. Here again, Hitler, who by now fancied himself a military genius without peer, did the unexpected.

On the German-French border was a wooded, hilly area called the Ardennes. French defenses along the Ardennes were relatively light because tanks could not possibly drive through it, or so the French thought. Hitler, supported this time by a key general, thought otherwise. On May 10, the same day Winston Churchill replaced Neville Chamberlain as prime minister of Britain, the Germans launched their offensive in the West. Airborne troops descended on Belgium and the Netherlands, as a German army headed for France by going around the northern end of the French defense system known as the Maginot Line. The Belgians and the Dutch were quickly conquered.

But the Germans' main thrust into France, a few days later, was through the Ardennes. German dive bombers called Stukas, equipped with screaming devices to terrify people on the ground, zoomed over France to soften up French defenses. Then the massive tank force burst through French ground defenses at a weak point west of the Maginot Line and dashed west toward the English Channel. The Allies, who had rushed troops north to fight the Germans in Belgium, were caught by surprise.

By May 20 the Germans had cut off Allied forces in the north from their bases in France. Trapped against the coast at Dunkirk, France, 340,000 British and French troops had only one way to escape— across the English Channel. Quibbling among Hitler and his military chiefs gave them their chance. While the German drive was stalled, boats of all sizes and shapes swarmed to Dunkirk to pick up Allied troops. By June 4 the evacuation had been completed. Arms and equipment were left behind, but most of the men were rescued. Historians consider Germany's failure to halt the rescue to be one of its greatest blunders in the war.

The rout of France began on June 5, 1940, with German attacks along the Somme River. On June 14, the Germans occupied Paris, and the swastika was raised over the Eiffel Tower. By June 22 it was all over. Hitler insisted that the French sign the armistice in the same railroad car, at the same spot in the woods at Compiègne, where the Germans had surrendered at the end of World War I. He had army engineers haul the car out of a museum for the occasion.

The next day, Hitler visited Paris for the first and only time. The lovely French capital dazzled him, and the man who now controlled much of Europe re-marked that just seeing this city fulfilled a lifelong dream of his. But sentimentality quickly gave way to ego. Hitler told his architect that Berlin must be re-built to be even more magnificent and to make all the other beautiful cities of Europe look insignificant.

Hitler still hoped for peace with Britain, but be-fore the summer of 1940 was over, he saw that the British were not interested in being his friends. Ger-man troops in June had captured the Channel Islands, which belong to Britain but are closer to the coast of France. In August, the Luftwaffe opened an attack on England intended to clear the way for an invasion. The Luftwaffe mauled the British Royal Air Force (RAF) fighters at first. Then Hitler and Göring made a tactical error. It began with an accident. On the night of August 23, a few German pilots trying to

Hitler dances with joy over his victory in
France at his headquartes in Compiègne
on June 17, 1940. The French would remain
under Nazi control for more than four years.

bomb factories on London's outskirts hit the center of the city by mistake. The British retaliated by bombing Berlin.

This was more than Hitler could bear. Never had bombs fallen on the Fatherland's capital. Britain would have to pay for this outrage. So on September 7, the Luftwaffe turned away from military targets and began fifty-seven days of pounding London, giving the battered RAF a chance to regroup. Other British cities were bombed, too, but neither morale nor arms production in Britain was destroyed. The planned invasion of Britain was called off. Defeat in the Battle of Britain was Hitler's first major loss.

Hitler and his staff were already at work on plans for the invasion of the Soviet Union. With its immense natural resources, the Soviet Union was critical to the German war effort and to Hitler's plans for feeding Germans in his empire. It also held the routes to the rich oil fields of the Middle East. No one could carry out a plan for conquest without fuel and raw materials to keep planes, tanks, and factories running.

Hitler pulled together a set of alliances in preparation for Operation Barbarossa, the attack on the Soviet Union. On September 27, 1940, Germany, Italy, and Japan joined in the Tripartite Pact, an agreement that Germany and Italy should dominate Europe, and Japan should dominate Asia. Romania was brought into the military alliance, the Axis Pact. Hitler invited Stalin to join the Tripartite Pact, which would essentially divide the world into spheres of influence for the four nations, but Stalin balked. Hitler had waited long enough. In December 1940, he ordered preparations for a spring invasion. One quick, massive attack would knock out the Soviets, he was certain. He would capture Moscow by the end of summer, then destroy the Soviet Union's leadership and enslave its people. He set the date of the invasion for May 15, 1941.

But to Hitler's great annoyance, he had to send troops south that spring to help Mussolini. The Italian dictator, incensed with his German ally's practice of occupying countries and then notifying Mussolini afterward, was trying some conquests of his own in Greece and North Africa, with disastrous results. German troops heading for Greece to bail out the Italians had to first travel through Hungary, Romania, Bulgaria, and Yugoslavia. The first three proved no problem, but Hitler became impatient at some political turmoil within Yugoslavia and ordered that that nation be destroyed. Hitler's troops then drove the Allies out of Greece and pushed the British back to Egypt. The cost of this adventure was enormous. The invasion of Russia had to be delayed by more than a month.

Then, on June 22, 1941, more than three million troops, or about four fifths of the German Army, plunged into what would become a long and indescribably brutal conflict. Soldiers were ordered to forget about the usual international rules of warfare, rules the Germans were observing in the West. The war in the East was to be a war of annihilation. Even civilians and prisoners of war were to be slaughtered. In the opening months the Germans seemed to be winning. On October 9, Hitler declared the Soviet Union beaten. He couldn't have been more wrong.

That month, the harsh Russian winter began. Hitler had made no provision for fighting in cold weather. He hadn't thought there would be any need.

In late November the temperature hit minus 36 degrees Fahrenheit. German troops trying to capture Moscow fought on frozen ground, in summer uniforms, and with equipment that could not stand up to the cold. Food supplies ran short. Some of the wounded ended up stranded on hospital trains that couldn't move because of the cold and snow. The Germans got no farther than the Soviet capital's outer suburbs. In early December the Soviets counterattacked and began to push the Germans back at last. All hope of an easy victory vanished.

Hitler's generals wanted to retreat, but the Führer wouldn't hear of it. He ordered that the army fight off the Russian offensive. Despite heavy losses, German forces managed to hold important ground throughout that winter. Hitler had shown his generals that iron will and a stubborn refusal to quit could overcome impossible odds.

Yet another development in December 1941 changed the complexion of the war. Japan bombed American ships at Pearl Harbor, Hawaii, on December 7. The next day, American President Franklin D. Roosevelt declared war on Japan, and on December 11, Hitler declared war on the United States. For the second time in the twentieth century, European conflict had become world war.

HOLOCAUST

7

The nationalization of our masses
will succeed only when, aside from
the positive struggle for the soul
of our people, their international
poisoners are exterminated.

ADOLF HITLER
MEIN KAMPF

These Hungarian Jews have just arrived at the Auschwitz extermination camp. It is unlikely that any of these women and children survived.

WHILE THE MIGHTY German military flexed its muscles across Europe, another killing campaign was going on within the territories that were under German rule. Government-sponsored murder on a massive scale was aimed at a group from which some of Europe's greatest thinkers, artists, and statesmen had come: the Jews.

In a speech to the Reichstag on January 30, 1939, Hitler had made his intentions clear: "If the Jewish international financiers succeed in involving the nations in another war, the result will not be world Bolshevism and therefore a victory for Judaism; it will be the destruction of the Jews in Europe."[1]

Hitler's drive to wipe out European Jews has come to be known as the Holocaust. Its unprecedented horror led to the coining of a new word: genocide, meaning the systematic attempt to destroy an entire race of people. Nazis referred to the victims as "useless eaters" or "life unworthy of life." It is fitting to begin a discussion of the Holocaust with a look at words. Words were an essential part of the killing operation.

By the fall of 1939, those Jews who had stayed in Germany were largely concentrated in big cities and had been stripped of many civil rights. When the war started, Jews were ordered to be off the streets by 8:00 P.M., and city police officers restricted Jews' movements. Eventually more identification requirements were piled on: On March 11, 1940, the government ordered that a red *J* be stamped on the ID cards used by Jews to get food rations. A September 1, 1941, decree required Jews over age six to wear a Jewish star with the word Jude (Jew) in the center. The next year, Jews were told to post a star on their apartment doors.

During this time, the "mercy killing" program was being carried on in nursing homes and mental hospitals throughout Germany. Jewish patients did not need to be certified mentally ill to be killed; it was enough that they were Jewish. But when word of the killing got out, the German public, some Christian leaders, and even party members raised objections. A group of mothers marched to the headquarters of the Gestapo and protested. Faced with this public outcry, Hitler called an official end to the program in August 1941. But the state-sanctioned killing of innocent people was just beginning.

Before resorting to systematic murder on a large scale, the Nazis simply tried to get the Jews out of

Europe. They hatched an ambitious plan in 1940 to ship millions of Jews to the island of Madagascar, off the eastern coast of Africa. The project would be paid for with wealth stolen from the Jews being deported. But several problems arose. For one thing, the island was under French control, and the French government objected. Furthermore, moving so many people so far would have required more transportation resources than Germany could spare. In 1941 the Nazis turned their attention to the invasion of the Soviet Union, and the scheme died. The Madagascar plan was Germany's last major effort to get rid of the Jews by emigration.

Meanwhile, with most of Poland under German rule, the Germans began rounding up Jews and herding them toward the area of Poland called the General Government. About two million Jews already lived in German-controlled Poland. Hans Frank, the Nazi in charge of the General Government, complained about his territory being a dumping ground for people the Nazis found undesirable. He urged that some other solution be found. Before long, his wish would be granted, with the Nazis' "Final Solution."

Moving toward that end, the Nazis created Jewish ghettos, or areas where only Jews would live, in the General Government and other Nazi-held areas. They moved the non-Jewish population out and forced Jews into the ghettos, which were primarily near rail lines in large cities. The first major ghetto, in Lodz, Poland, was set up in April 1940. Warsaw, which had a Jewish population of several hundred thousand before the Nazis arrived, saw the initiation of its ghetto in October 1940. Most other ghettos were in place by the end of 1941.

By this time, Jews had been gradually separated from non-Jews—socially, economically, and physically. Thus isolated, they could be more easily deported or slaughtered. Hitler and his henchmen were keenly aware of the need to remove Jews from Germany without sparking public outrage. They planned to commit the most gruesome of their crimes in the occupied territories in the East, out of view of the German public.

Conditions in the ghettos spelled death for many Jews. The Nazi masters let in only meager food supplies, and hunger and disease claimed thousands of lives. An estimated 45,000 people died in the Lodz ghetto and about 83,000 in Warsaw. Birthrates plummeted. But the Nazis couldn't wait for Jews to die off slowly. So they turned to quicker and more direct methods of killing.

THE "FINAL SOLUTION." When Germany invaded the Soviet Union on June 22, 1941, small SS squads were sent in behind the army. Their mission was to locate Jews and kill them on the spot. These roving death units were called Einsatzgruppen, literally "action squads." Whole villages were burned, entire Jewish communities taken out and shot. Hitler's goal in the East was not just to win the war but to annihilate millions—Communists, Jews, Slavs, and Gypsies.

Jews in the Soviet Union had not fared well under the Communists, and many actually welcomed the Nazis, believing that the Germans would prove better rulers than those they had. Einsatzgruppen leaders took full advantage of this misplaced trust. They gathered large groups of Jews with simple ruses, calling them together for "registration" or "resettlement." The tricks worked time and again.

Many Soviet Jews, who had suffered terribly under Joseph Stalin and his Communist regime, hoped that the Nazi invasion might bring relief. These are only six of the half-million Soviet Jews killed by the Einsatz-gruppen under Hitler's orders.

In a secluded spot outside of town, a huge grave would be waiting. Victims were divided into smaller groups and told to hand over valuables and sometimes clothing. Killing squads lined up the Jews at the edge of the ditch and shot them in the back of the neck, letting the bodies tumble in. Blood splattered on the uniforms of the shooters. Sometimes Jews were killed in a system called the "sardine method." Victims were forced to lie down in the grave and were shot from above. The next group had to lie on top of the bleeding bodies, some of which still writhed and twitched with life. The new group put their heads at the feet of those below. When the dead and dying were five or six deep, the grave was covered with dirt.

Within five months, the roving death squads had murdered 500,000 Jews. Einsatzgruppen commanders gave their men extra rations of liquor, food, and cigarettes. Many of the men who wielded the guns were sickened by their task, and most drank themselves into a stupor before mass executions. Some committed suicide, and others went insane. Even the cold-blooded SS chief Heinrich Himmler nearly fainted the first time he witnessed a mass shooting, in the summer of 1941. He returned to Berlin and ordered that more humane methods of murder be found.

The result of Himmler's order was the use of gas vans. Victims were loaded into a sealed van, and deadly carbon monoxide from the engine's exhaust was pumped in. By the time the vehicle arrived at a waiting mass grave, the van was full of corpses. Just how much killing the Nazis could do with poison gas remained to be seen.

It was apparently sometime in the summer of 1941 that Hitler told Himmler to find a permanent "solution." This marked the Nazis' move from mass murder into genocide. No document bearing Hitler's signature has ever been turned up linking the Führer explicitly to the plan for genocide, which the Nazis referred to as the "final solution to the Jewish problem." But by the end of that summer, Göring and Reich security chief Reinhard Heydrich were both talking about a "Führer order" on the matter. And Göring, asked after the war who had been responsible for the camps, replied: "Hitler personally. Everyone who had anything to do with the camps was directly responsible to Hitler."[2]

Göring directed Heydrich on July 31, 1941, to come up with "a total solution of the Jewish question within the German sphere of influence in Europe."[3] Rumors were already circulating among the public that the Nazis had a plan to exterminate the Jews. That fall, Hitler remarked to Himmler and Heydrich, the two SS leaders with greatest responsibility for the program, that he didn't mind the rumors. The terror they inspired, he said, was a healthy thing.

Heydrich called a "Final Solution" conference of fifteen Nazi leaders in January 1942 in the Berlin suburb of Wannsee. There, he explained his plan: The remaining Jews were to be rounded up and sent to work camps. Those who could not work would be killed immediately. Those who could work would be worked to death. And anyone strong enough to survive such harsh treatment clearly represented a danger to Germany and would have to be "treated accordingly." This meant "killed," and everyone present knew it. Now, instead of the slower and less efficient methods of killing already in use, the Nazis had a systematic plan for mass exterminations.

Responsibility for putting the plan into action fell to Adolf Eichmann, head of Jewish affairs throughout German-controlled territory. Eichmann was perfect for the job: He was obsessed with killing every Jew he could get his hands on. The Gestapo was put in charge of the roundups, and it enlisted the aid of the SA, the SS, local police, and even Jewish leaders.

In retrospect, and knowing what fate awaited the Jews, it may be hard to imagine why the Jews did not resist the Nazis more forcefully. The reasons are complex. For one thing, most were trapped in overcrowded ghettos, hungry and unarmed. Also, because the Nazis had so thoroughly isolated them, the Jews were easily deceived. No one knew what lay ahead. Rumors circulated, especially in Poland, where the Nazis built their most notorious killing camps, but most Jews did not grasp the enormity of the Nazi plan. They could not believe that the government of a civilized, modern nation would embark on a program to wipe them out. Instead, they clung to the hope that by cooperating they could make it easier on themselves. Resistance, many Jewish leaders believed, would only bring greater harm to the entire Jewish community. By the time Jews did organize and fight back, it was too late.

THE CAMPS. Jewish leaders supplied the Nazis with maps and name lists and even helped round up and supervise Jews being deported. Few managed to escape or hide for long. The Gestapo hauled Jews through the streets in open trucks, so crowds could jeer at the deportees, then packed them into freight cars for the long, slow ride to their doom. The cars were sealed shut, and captives trapped inside them went days at a time without food or water. Some suffocated. The deportees were forced to pay the cost of their final journey.

Their destinations were the extermination camps that Heydrich had envisioned. The first death camp, Chelmno, opened in December 1941. Eventually there were six, all in rural Poland. Sites were chosen that were secluded but close to rail lines. Jewish slave laborers did much of the construction work. Then trains on strict schedules brought Jewish victims by the thousands to camps at Chelmno, Belzec, Sobibor, Maidanek, Treblinka, and the killing center whose name has become synonymous with Nazi genocide: Auschwitz.

The Nazis carried their deception of Jews right to the end. Camps were designed to look like transit stations, with flowering plants about the platform and an orchestra playing for new arrivals. An official greeted them with a soothing speech, saying they would get job training in the camp before being resettled. First, though, they must be bathed and disinfected. Belongings were collected and claim checks handed out, and the Jews were sent to what looked like shower rooms. But the buildings were gas chambers in disguise. At first, Jews were gassed with carbon monoxide—engine exhaust. Later, Auschwitz commander Rudolf Höss introduced a more effective gas.

In his postwar confession to the Allies, Höss gave this chilling account:

> When I set up the extermination building at Auschwitz, I used Zyklon B, which was a crystallized prussic acid which we dropped into the death chamber from a small opening. It took from three to 15 minutes to kill the people in the death chamber. . . . We knew when the people were dead because their screaming stopped. . . . Another improvement we made over Treblinka was that we built our gas chambers to accommodate 2,000 people at one time. . . . The foul and nauseating

stench from the continuous burning of bodies permeated the entire area and all of the people living in the surrounding communities knew that exterminations were going on.4

Höss built a huge camp that was an industrial complex as well as a death center. When a trainload of Jews arrived, everyone had to walk down a ramp leading into the camp, where a doctor would perform the "selection"—he would indicate with the flick of a finger who would be gassed immediately and who would be spared for the moment. The old, the sick, and small children were separated out to be killed first. Most were dead within two hours of their arrival. Jews who survived the first selection were put to work. These laborers generally survived for about three months. At its peak, Auschwitz was killing 20,000 people a day.

Most notorious among the doctors of Auschwitz was Joseph Mengele. Handsome, dapper, always immaculately groomed, Mengele was known as the Angel of Death. He whistled while doing ramp selections. Mengele made a specialty of torturing children, calling the sadistic treatments medical experiments. Mengele was particularly fond of twins, thinking he might learn from his experiments how to reproduce the "master race" in greater numbers. He spoke soothingly to his twin-victims, and some even called him Uncle Mengele. He injected them with a variety of substances, drew fluids from their bodies, stood them on their heads or dunked them in cold water until they passed out. He injected dyes into children's eyes to see if he could turn brown eyes blue. His cruelty was far from unique.

Nazi doctors in Auschwitz and other camps used inmates as guinea pigs for a mind-boggling array of experiments. Male and female inmates were sterilized in lightning-quick operations with little or no anesthesia. They were put in pressure chambers from which the oxygen was slowly removed until they died grisly deaths. Some were shot with poison bullets. Others were injected with deadly diseases, or cut open and given infections with dirt or glass so the doctors could test treatments. Organs were removed from living prisoners for study. Nazi doctors cut arms and legs off healthy inmates and tried grafting them onto other prisoners. The skin of camp inmates was made into purses, gloves, and lampshades. Some inmates were carefully measured, then killed so their skeletons could be sent to a research institution. This killing was often done by a lethal phenol injection into the heart; the practice was called "spritzen," or squirting, and its victims were said to have been "abgespritzt," or squirted off.

Where did all those bodies go? At first, victims were buried in mass graves. But the decomposing bodies swelled, stank, and drew bugs and rodents. They were dug up and burned in pits. Then Höss devised another "improvement"—compact units with gas chambers and cremation ovens in the same building.

Before the last roll call on January 17, 1945, at Auschwitz, gas chambers there had killed more than a million people from all over Europe. Altogether, the Nazi program of genocide is believed to have been responsible for the deaths of about 6 million Jews. (Historians disagree on the number of Jews killed by the Germans and their allies. Estimates range from

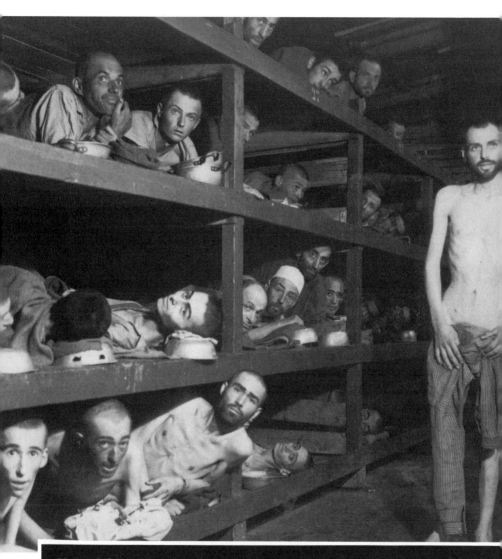

United States troops came upon these slave laborers in the Buchenwald concentration camp in Germany in 1945.

about 5.6 million to 6.9 million. Research continues.) Others killed in Nazi camps included about 3 million Soviet prisoners of war, 3 million Polish leaders and intellectuals, and 300,000 to 1 million Gypsies.

Adolf Hitler, the man behind the murders, delegated the operation of the Nazi killing machine. So far as is known, he never watched a mass execution or visited a death camp. But aides in his inner circle had no doubt about what the Führer wanted. And they did their best to give it to him. In the years and decades to come, they would learn that claiming they had just followed orders did not excuse them for murdering millions.

Can the bloodguilt of the Holocaust be placed only on those who had a direct hand in the killing? Should the camp construction crews, the Zyklon B suppliers, the railroad operators, the office-bound bureaucrats, and the residents who smelled the smoke of burning corpses share the blame? Could the leaders of Allied nations that did not stop Hitler sooner also be held culpable?

The memory of Hitler's Holocaust would color Germany's domestic politics and international relations for decades. Perhaps there is no such thing as collective guilt. But for Germans, despite the passing of time, there would most certainly remain such a thing as collective shame.

8

There are two possibilities for me:
to win through with all my plans,
or to fail. If I win, I shall be one of
the greatest men in history.

If I fail, I shall be condemned,
despised, and damned.

ADOLF HITLER
NOVEMBER 1936

After months of brutal hand-to-hand combat throughout Stalingrad, it was the harsh Russian winter as much as the strength of Soviet resistance that brought the German offensive to its knees. Here, defeated German soldiers trudge through the snow to prisoner-of-war camps.

THE ATROCITIES OF THE
Nazi camps could be hidden while the world's attention was on the war, and especially while Germany was dominating the conflict. Hitler had already planted the seeds of his own defeat, however, by failing to mobilize the German economy for war. His military and his people would soon reap what their Führer had sown.

Hitler had never had formal military training. Once his Blitzkrieg tactics began to fail, the results of this lack showed. The man who almost twenty years earlier had organized the Nazi party with such skill and foresight proved himself to be fatally shortsighted at organizing a war effort.

For one thing, an army fighting a long war needs tremendous support. Weapons, ammunition, tanks, and planes have to be built and then transported to the men who use them. Food, clothing, fuel, and other supplies have to be organized for the fighting troops. Bridges, railroad tracks, roads, and airfields have to be repaired quickly, or troops can't move. Spare parts have to be manufactured and made easily available for use on the front. These are tedious but critical details, and Hitler had little interest in them.

Another of Hitler's failures was the way he had his army and the SS treat people in the conquered territories. In Eastern Europe and the Soviet Union, the Nazis had a chance to make allies of the native people who had suffered under Stalin's domination. And in Poland, despite its large Jewish population, there was a history of anti-Semitism. If the Germans had tried to win over these conquered peoples, Hitler could have had an important source of labor and military recruits. Instead, the Nazis treated the Slavs brutally, sometimes wiping out whole villages on flimsy pretexts. Millions were dragged from their homes and sent to Germany to work as slaves. Inevitably, the Nazis managed to inspire in the conquered people a loyalty to the Communists that they had not felt before.

The year 1942 was one of victories for Hitler, but also one of increasing difficulty. Germany gained control of much of North Africa, and German submarines sank British and American ships in the Atlantic faster than the Allies could replace them. By late summer, the Axis powers held much of the northern and southern shores of the Mediterranean as well as territory north to the Arctic Circle, west to the Atlantic Ocean, and east to the Volga River. But Allied bombers by the thousands rained destruction on Germany, beginning with a 1,000-bomber RAF raid on Cologne in May. Other cities were also pummeled, and with them German morale, while Göring and the Luftwaffe seemed powerless to stop the attacks.

Hitler remained confident that he could win the war, if only by sheer force of will. After all, he had held out against the Soviets the previous winter when his generals wanted to retreat. In the summer of 1942, he felt ready to finish off the Soviets. At first, he planned a rapid drive toward Stalingrad, on the Volga River, and then a push toward the oil-rich Caucasus region. But ultimately, he was so sure the Soviets were too weak to fight back that he ordered both campaigns to be carried out at once. Hard-eyed realism had no place in Hitler's planning now. He refused to listen to his military advisers' predictions that he was marching into disaster. With the Battle of Stalingrad, the war would turn, once and for all.

On September 13, 1942, the German Sixth Army launched its attack on Stalingrad. Stalin was determined to defend the city that bore his name; Hitler was equally determined to capture it. Fierce fighting raged from street to street, house to house, sometimes room to room. Battles were fought and refought over the same patch of ground. German generals warned Hitler that he should quit, but Hitler refused. For a while, it seemed the Germans could take Stalingrad. But then Stalin put together a force of more than one million troops and surrounded the city. By late November, the Germans were trapped.

Hitler's generals pleaded with him to let the Sixth Army try to break out of Stalingrad and flee. The Führer refused. His men must take Stalingrad or die trying. Göring, by now feeling he had to prove himself because his Luftwaffe was failing so miserably at stopping Allied bombing raids, promised Hitler that he could airlift enough supplies to the Stalingrad troops. He didn't even come close. Toward the end of the year, the Germans made one last effort to reach Stalingrad and rescue the troops there. The Soviets stopped the drive in its tracks.

On January 24, 1943, General Friedrich Paulus, leader of the Stalingrad troops, begged for permission to surrender. He described the situation bluntly: No ammunition, no food, no medical supplies for the 18,000 wounded soldiers. "Further defense senseless. Collapse inevitable," Paulus said.[1] Hitler forbade surrender. This time, though, his military men defied him and gave up anyway.

Thus, in the first week of February 1943, did the Battle of Stalingrad end. About two thirds of the 300,000 German troops sent to Stalingrad had been killed, and the Luftwaffe managed to evacuate about 29,000 wounded. The rest were marched off to prisoner-of-war (POW) camps. Only about 5,000 Germans survived to see their homeland again.

Around the same time, German troops in North Africa were meeting with their own disaster. Hitler's plan had been to push south through the Caucasus and meet up with Axis troops heading east across North Africa. But in the fall of 1942, British forces defeated the Germans at El Alamein, Egypt, and shortly afterward Allied troops landed in Northwest Africa. By the end of the spring of 1943, the Germans had been driven from the African continent. About 140,000 Germans and as many Italians were hauled off to POW camps. And the Allies were in a position to menace the Axis powers from the south.

Throughout 1943, Germany was beaten back on several fronts. A July offensive against the Soviet Union around Kursk threw half a million Germans into a tank battle that ended in defeat in a matter of weeks. The Soviets retook the Ukraine and kept pushing the Germans back all along the battlefront. The German submarine fleet was knocked out in the Atlantic. American bombers raided German cities by day, and British bombers pounded them by night. Allied attacks on Hamburg ignited the city, creating a firestorm so fierce that even the asphalt in the streets blazed. In Italy, Mussolini was driven from office and arrested by his own people. British and American troops landed on Sicily and forced Germans there to flee to the Italian mainland.

Because of the extent and depth of evil that Hitler unleashed on the world, it would be easy to think of him as something other than a human being. But he was human, and as 1943 wore on it became clear to everyone around him that Hitler was falling apart.

Nightmares haunted him after Stalingrad. His moods swung wildly, and he was plagued with stomach cramps, headaches that lasted for days, insomnia, and a tremor in an arm and a leg. He began each day with an amphetamine injection before he got out of bed, then took several more shots throughout the day. He may have had a mild heart attack in the spring or summer of 1943.

Perpetual suspicion colored Hitler's dealings with aides, and he turned for advice only to those who would offer optimistic assurances. Where he had previously assigned others to look after details, he now wanted to make even the smallest decisions himself. He refused to visit the bombed cities or the battlefront, trying instead to run the war by consulting his maps. He talked of developing a secret weapon that would turn things around and still hoped the British would join Germany in a fight against communism. Hitler became more unpredictable than ever and refused to listen to any opposition to his decisions. When confronted with information about rising Allied arms production, he dismissed the reports as propaganda. His orders became so bizarre that even Himmler remarked that Hitler was mentally sick.

By now, the battle instincts Hitler had always relied on were of no use whatsoever. Hitler had not understood the logistics of getting arms from the factories to the troops. German supply lines were hopelessly overextended. As a result, although German factories were producing plenty of ammunition, soldiers in the trenches were running out.

THE NOOSE TIGHTENS. Early 1944 found the British and Americans slowly pushing north through Italy and the Soviets taking back territory in the East. On June 4, 1944, the Allies captured Rome. But the decisive Allied return to the European continent occurred two days later. On June 6, 1944, the Allies finally opened the second front that Hitler had feared with the invasion of the continent from the north. Making their D-Day incursion at Normandy, on the northern coast of France, the Allies surprised Hitler and his generals. The Germans had anticipated the invasion, but they had thought it would take place at Calais, where the English Channel was narrowest. Sure that the Normandy landing was a decoy, Hitler waited more than three weeks before he agreed to move troops from Calais to help the swamped soldiers fighting near Normandy. By then it was too late. As Allied troops poured ashore in the West that summer, the Soviets tore apart the German front in the East.

Hitler's generals became louder and more bitter in their criticism of him. For some time, he had infuriated them by reversing their orders and meddling in defense production plans. Finally, a few German officers decided they had had enough and plotted to assassinate the Führer. On July 20, 1944, Colonel Claus von Stauffenberg brought a briefcase containing a time bomb to Hitler's daily military conference, then made an excuse and left. Minutes later, the bomb exploded, shattering the room, flinging bodies and debris, and killing several men. Hitler emerged from the wreckage shaken, dust-covered, and slightly injured—but alive.

Now he was more convinced than ever that he was destined to carry out his mission. He installed Nazi political officers in military offices and ordered the army to start using the Nazi party salute. Hitler vowed revenge on the conspirators, and throughout the rest of the war they, their families, and thousands of others suspected of opposing the Nazis would be hunted down and sent to camps or executed.

That summer, Hitler's world shriveled like a grape in the sun. The Soviets liberated the first of the death camps, Maidanek, in July. In August, Allied forces liberated Paris and pushed the Germans out of the Balkans, Germany's main source of oil. By the end of that month, the Soviets were 400 miles (644 kilometers) east of Berlin, and Allied troops were about 500 miles (805 kilometers) west of it. On September 11, Americans crossed the border into Germany, bringing the ground war onto German soil.

Hitler refused to take the blame for the catastrophe befalling Germany. The army, an organization of traitors and cowards, was at fault, he concluded. In October 1944, he created a party-controlled force consisting of every able-bodied male between the ages of sixteen and sixty to defend the Fatherland. Predictably, the untrained and ill-equipped Volkssturm, or People's Storm, accomplished nothing.

Desperate, scratching frantically for any shred of hope, Hitler decided that a bold, surprising move was called for, the kind that had won him such astonishing victories at the start. He ordered a new attack through the Ardennes, where German troops had succeeded so grandly in 1940, with the aim of capturing the Belgian port the Allies relied on for supplies. But Germany no longer had the resources for such an ambitious attack, and the generals knew it.

As always, the Führer dismissed their objections. On December 16, 1944, Germany surprised the Allies with this new Ardennes offensive (also called the Battle of the Bulge). The Germans inflicted heavy losses on the Allies, but Hitler's generals had been right. By Christmas, it was clear the attack had failed. In January 1945, Hitler authorized a retreat. Tens of thousands of lives had been lost—for nothing.

TWILIGHT OF THE REICH

**Just think. Three years ago
Hitler had Europe under his
command, from the Volga to
the Atlantic. Now he's sitting
in a hole under the earth.**

GENERAL
GOTTHARD HEINRICI

MARCH 1945

Hitler and his entourage study the
effects of Allied bombing in Germany;
the tide of the war has turned.

HITLER WAS A WRECK.

His face was ashen, his voice hoarse. His hands shook, his stomach ached, and he stooped when he walked. He relied on amphetamine injections to keep him going in the daytime and barbiturates to put him to sleep at night. His eyes often filled with tears. He spent most of his time holed up in his windowless bunker under the Chancellery in Berlin, constantly in fear of another assassination attempt.

The bunker, with its walls 16 feet (4.8 meters) thick, had barely been finished. Fire hoses along the ground served as water pipes, and the rooms still smelled of damp plaster. Here, in this tomblike shelter, Hitler inched closer to death, day by day. Everyone around him could see the Führer had lost contact with reality. He told his military advisers that anyone caught saying the war was lost would be severely punished, and he had Gestapo chief Ernst Kaltenbrunner sit in on meetings to underscore the point. Those who received field reports from the army saw that sharing the details with Hitler was pointless, so they stopped telling him the truth. At his daily military conferences, Hitler talked of smashing the enemy with planes that did not exist and bombs that did not work.

And as the man disintegrated, so did his authority. Party district leaders, or Gauleiters, stopped trains carrying coal and other materials and confiscated whatever they wanted for themselves. Military commanders in the field began to disregard orders that they knew would only result in useless sacrifice of lives. Hitler's commands were more and more frequently ignored at all levels. After the Russians all but shattered the eastern German line in January 1945, one general actually got into a public shouting match with the Führer.

By early 1945, Hitler had decided that the German people who had failed him so miserably were not worth saving. Let them be crushed, they deserved it, he said. Hitler ordered that everything his nation would need in order to rebuild after the war— communications, utilities, industry, transportation— be destroyed. There should be nothing left of Germany but a desert. Albert Speer, Hitler's armaments minister and one of his closest aides, traveled the country trying to countermand this scorched-earth order. Some party loyalists tried to carry out the Führer's decree, but defiance was everywhere.

Even Hitler's oldest cronies could no longer hold his respect. He berated Göring in front of the military chiefs during situation conferences, blaming him for the Luftwaffe's inability to turn the war around. Himmler also fell from favor. He assumed command of an army group in the East, taking on the impossible job of stopping the Russian advance. When he inevitably failed, Hitler became abusive with him, too.

THE ALLIES CLOSE IN. Meanwhile, in February 1945, the Allies' Big Three—Stalin, Churchill, and Roosevelt—had their last wartime conference, at Yalta, in the Soviet Union. A secret plan for the postwar occupation of Germany by the three powers had been drawn up in November 1944. Now these leaders decided that France should also be a partner in occupying Germany and Berlin. At the meeting's end, the Allies repeated their demand for unconditional surrender. Hitler and his advisers had waited and hoped for the alliance among Germany's enemies to fall apart. The Yalta communiqué made it clear that this was not going to happen. The political front against Germany was still solid.

In the spring of 1945 the Allies bombed Germany's industrial areas relentlessly. Day after day, waves of bombers roared over Berlin. The Luftwaffe had neither planes nor fuel to fight back. What was left of the ground forces were remnants of army and SS units, some pro-Nazi volunteers from other countries, Hitler Youth boys, old men, and even some former Soviet POWs who had been talked into forming an anti-Stalinist unit. On the whole, they were disorganized, ill-equipped, largely untrained, and virtually without capable leadership.

Allied troops closed in on Berlin like a vise; British and American forces pressed the German empire from the West, Soviet troops from the East. Party bureaucrats packed their belongings and families into cars and fled on the clogged roads leading out of the capital. Anglo-American troops met scattered resistance, but in town after town they found residents hanging out white flags, sheets, or whatever fabric they could find to signal their surrender. In some villages, the residents begged German soldiers to stay out of their towns. They didn't want any pointless fighting now.

The eastern front was another matter. After the terrible war of annihilation the Germans had waged against the Soviet Union, the Soviets were bent on revenge. Terrified refugees poured into Berlin, bringing stories of murder, rape, looting, and wild, drunken orgies. Many tried to commit suicide to escape the torture they feared from the Soviets.

The Allies barreling toward Berlin now began stumbling onto the evidence of Nazi genocide. The Soviets had already suffered enormously at the hands of the Nazis and knew what cruelty they were capable of. But when Anglo-American soldiers on their push eastward discovered concentration camps—the walking skeletons, the mass graves, the gas chambers still full of bodies, the crematoria, the efficiently sorted possessions of the dead and dying stored in warehouses, the survivors packed into huts along with corpses—many became ill. Even hard-bitten American General George S. Patton was reduced to tears. He ordered the entire population of one village to view a nearby camp. General Dwight D. Eisenhower, the Allied commander, toured one of the liberated camps, seeing what the man who caused so much misery never saw for himself.

As the Soviets moved westward, the Nazis frantically tried to dismantle the death camps' gas chambers, destroy the evidence of what they had done, and get the remaining inmates out. Many prisoners who had held on this long waiting for liberation died on these final marches. Others were dumped into camps within Germany and left to be attacked by rats or to die of starvation or typhus. The men responsible for the killing scrambled. Some killed themselves, some hid or fled, others surrendered. Eichmann ordered Höss to make sure no inmates survived. He told the camp commandant: "No one will walk out of Auschwitz. There is only one way they will leave—through the smokestacks."[1] Then he vanished.

THE FALL OF BERLIN. The Nazis had one last fleeting moment of hope when American President Roosevelt died on April 12. Goebbels was ecstatic. He phoned Hitler in the bunker the next day to shout his congratulations and declared that April 13—Friday the thirteenth—would mark a turning point in the war. Hitler called his aides together and crowed that a miracle was at hand. But nothing changed.

On April 16, 1945, the Battle of Berlin began. Flares lighted the predawn sky as the Soviets opened the greatest bombardment the eastern front had seen. Hitler had declared the city to be a fortress, but the impregnable defenses existed only in his imagination. Old men, whose "uniforms" consisted of armbands sewn on jacket sleeves, tried to dig trenches with hand tools. A grim joke went: "It will take the Reds at least two hours and 15 minutes to break through. Two hours laughing their heads off, and 15 minutes smashing the barricades."[2] Within a week, the fighting reached the streets of the city.

Hitler had decided to kill himself rather than survive to be captured. Eva Braun would join him, he said, and he would kill his dog, Blondi. By this time, Hitler seemed a very old man. His feet dragged when he walked, and he trembled more than ever. The uniform he had always kept immaculate now often carried the evidence of spilled food, and he had to use a rubber stamp to sign his name.

On April 20, as he had every year, Hitler gathered his party and military leaders to mark his birthday. This year, as the Führer turned fifty-six, it was hardly a celebration. He received a group of Hitler Youth boys and gave them a last pep talk, speaking softly and patting a couple. He pinned medals on some. Then the young men were dispatched to be slaughtered by the enemy, in the name of Hitler's lost cause. The Allies had another way of honoring the Führer on his birthday: They engulfed Berlin in five hours of air raids that day.

Over the next ten days, what remained of Hitler's world crumbled. When Göring, who had fled, heard that Hitler had had a breakdown, he sent a quick message asking for Hitler's agreement that he, Göring, should take over. He was promptly arrested for treason. Himmler, meanwhile, had been making secret peace overtures to the western Allies. When Hitler got word of this betrayal, he ordered Himmler arrested, too. Further, he learned that Mussolini had been caught and executed.

With the end in sight, Hitler focused on details and formalities. He went through piles of documents, selecting some to be burned. He made a little ceremony of handing out small containers of poison to the staff members left in the bunker. He left instructions for his body to be burned beyond recognition and had a will drawn up. Eva Braun had shown up at the bunker unexpectedly some days earlier, and now he

Hitler made his last public appearance on his fifty-sixth and final birthday, on April 20, 1945. He is congratulating members of the Hitler Youth for their bravery.

made his longstanding relationship with her legitimate. On April 29, as plaster fell from the bunker walls with each artillery shell's crash outside, Hitler married Braun, calling her "the woman who, after many years of true friendship, came to this city . . . to share my fate."[3]

Later, he dictated one final testament, his version of events. He asserted: "It is untrue that I or anybody else in Germany wanted war in 1939."[4] And, as always, he blamed Jews for everything: "Centuries may pass, but out of the ruins of our cities and cultural monuments hatred will again rise against the people who were ultimately responsible for our misery: international Jewry and its accomplices."[5]

The next day, Hitler and his new wife said their good-byes and retired to their suite. She took a fatal dose of poison, and the Führer shot himself in the head. Their bodies were taken into the Chancellery garden, soaked with gasoline, and burned. Goebbels had remained in the bunker, with his wife and six children. After Hitler's death, Goebbels and his wife poisoned their children, then committed suicide.

On May 7, 1945, Admiral Karl Dönitz, whom Hitler had named to succeed him, surrendered unconditionally to the Allies.

The Thousand-Year Reich was over.

And the Lord said unto Cain,
Where is Abel thy brother?

And he said, I know not:
Am I my brother's keeper?

And he said, What hast
thou done? the voice of thy
brother's blood crieth unto
me from the ground.

GENESIS 4: 9–10

More than 100,000 people gathered in New York City to protest the 1944 massacre of Jews in Hungary, the Balkans, and Eastern Europe. Global reaction to the atrocities committed by Hitler's regime was too little and too late.

ITH TWENTY-TWENTY hindsight, it is easy to look at what Hitler did and ask: How did he get away with it? Why didn't anyone stop him? Why didn't someone rescue the Jews?

The answers to these questions are not easy. Some Germans—Jewish and non-Jewish—resisted the Nazis, and some voices of outrage were raised in other countries. None of the protests stopped or even seriously slowed Hitler's march of conquest and killing. International politics played an important role, as did the political, social, and economic situations in other countries.

In the United States and Britain, the Versailles Treaty was widely viewed as unfair to Germany. France, which shared a border with Germany, did not agree with this view. But the French did share the other nations' desperate desire for peace. When Hitler was pushing forward with his bloodless conquests, the British and the French thought each concession they made would be the last. When British Prime Minister Neville Chamberlain allowed the carving up of Czechoslovakia, he was hailed in London because he seemed to have preserved peace. The United States, meanwhile, was determined not to get involved in another European dispute.

Hitler took advantage of these attitudes, talking about peace while trying to break up peacekeeping alliances. The 1936 Berlin Olympics, held soon after the Rhineland remilitarization, was Hitler's showcase of peace. Everyone wanted to believe it. Even Germans, united in their hatred of the Versailles Treaty, did not want to go to war over the settlement.

WHY THE WORLD TURNED AWAY. International reaction to the persecution of German Jews in the 1930s reflected both anti-immigrant feelings and anti-Semitism. The United States seemed an obvious place for the Jews to emigrate. But the United States was still suffering the effects of the Great Depression. Unemployment was high between 1933 and 1941, and many U.S. residents feared, as they do today, that immigrants would snap up jobs that should belong to Americans. American Jews were reluctant to stage protests, fearing that the Nazis would retaliate by striking German Jews. Public-opinion surveys in the United States showed a strong current of anti-Semitism and widespread unwillingness to let Hitler's victims in. American politicians, including President Roosevelt, didn't want to take action against the wishes of voters.

Kristallnacht, the night in 1938 when Nazi terror against Jews burst into international view, shocked the world. *The New York Times* published an editorial denouncing the violence, and President Roosevelt publicly condemned it. But three quarters of Americans were still opposed to opening the doors to German refugees.

In May 1939 a luxury cruise ship called the *St. Louis* left Hamburg, Germany, bound for Cuba with more than nine hundred Jewish refugees on it. But Cuba would not let the refugees land there and forced the ship out of Havana harbor. It steamed up and down the coast of Florida, while passengers hoped the United States would take them in. Again they were turned away. The *St. Louis* finally returned to Europe in June, letting off refugees in Holland, Belgium, France, and England. Many were later caught and killed by the Nazis.

British-controlled Palestine, where Israel was later founded, was another possible haven for threatened Jews. About 550,000 Jews already lived there in the 1930s and were willing to take in Jewish refugees. But the British did not want to anger Arab residents and in May 1939 imposed tight restrictions on Jewish immigration to Palestine. After that, shiploads of Jews reached Palestine only to be turned away. Some refugees who made it to shore were imprisoned, and others were expelled.

But it was during the war, when the state-directed killing turned into systematic genocide, that Hitler's victims most desperately needed help from the rest of the world.

In the first year of the war, Hitler pushed the British off the European continent and subdued the French. As Germany continued to dominate the war,

Jews were being concentrated in ghettos and camps. News of the Einsatzgruppen killings was broadcast in Moscow in the summer of 1941, and similar reports showed up in *The New York Times* that fall. As late as the fall of 1941, Jews could have escaped by emigrating if there had been anywhere they could go. Then, in January 1942, the "Final Solution" conference was held, formalizing the extermination plan.

Word of the plan reached the United States within months. In May 1942 a Jewish organization in Poland reported in detail on gassings at Chelmno and estimated that 700,000 Polish Jews had already been killed. Most important, it concluded that an effort was in progress to kill all European Jews. That August, a German industrialist told the U.S. government and American Jewish organizations that the Nazis had a plan to systematically wipe out Europe's Jews. The U.S. State Department dismissed the report as unbelievable. By this time, 2 million Jews had already been killed. Throughout that year, reports of deportations and slaughter filtered out to the West, from a variety of sources. One report named Treblinka, Belzec, and Sobibor as killing centers.

President Roosevelt, who was popular among American Jews, knew about the genocide by the end of 1942. News of the "Final Solution" was published in *The New York Times*. But the Allies took no action on the news.

Why? For one thing, the Holocaust was unfolding against the backdrop of war, and in 1942 the Germans were still winning. The United States, ill-prepared for a global conflict, was tied up fighting the Japanese in the Pacific. And in the November 1942 elections in the United States, immigration opponents gained a number of seats in Congress. They smashed efforts to open American doors. In addition, there was the problem of getting the Nazis to let Jews go. With Hitler controlling most of Europe, reaching potential victims was no simple matter for the Allies.

In February 1943, Romania offered to help evacuate 70,000 Jews to any place the Allies chose. The U.S. State Department rejected the offer, and the British likewise dismissed it. Jewish activists appealed to British Foreign Secretary Anthony Eden in March to try to get the remaining Jews out of Hitler's territory, or at least to send in supplies to help them. Eden rebuffed the plea—not because he thought such efforts would fail, but because he feared they might succeed. It was a fear the U.S. State Department shared: What if Hitler decided to let the Jews go? What could the Allies do with them?

By 1943 the American public was beginning to recognize what Hitler was doing. Anti-Hitler rallies drew thousands. Widespread calls for action finally prompted the Americans and the British to meet in April 1943 in Bermuda to discuss the refugee question. No representatives of Jewish groups were invited. The twelve-day-long Bermuda Conference degenerated into an argument over a few thousand refugees in Spain. Its one concrete result was a camp that opened months later in North Africa. About six hundred people found haven there. A newly established Intergovernmental Committee on Refugees, despite its impressive-sounding name, managed mostly to stall any proposals for rescue.

It wasn't only government agencies that were silent. Except for an outcry from some small denominations, Christian churches had little to say against Nazi genocide. Mainstream news media were also mostly quiet on the subject. Holocaust stories usually appeared far from the front pages of major U.S. newspapers—when they appeared at all.

The Jewish press gave heavy coverage to the tragedy in Europe, but political disagreements kept Jewish groups from uniting to take action. Some Jewish leaders wanted all possible efforts to be made to rescue Jews from the Nazis; others, called Zionists, thought the rescue cause was hopeless and that energy and money would be better spent working toward the establishment of a Jewish state after the war.

Within the U.S. government, officials quarreled over the rescue issue. Although the White House and the State Department stonewalled rescue efforts, the Treasury Department pushed for action. Pressure finally grew strong enough that in January 1944, President Roosevelt established the War Refugee Board, an agency whose job was to take concrete steps to help Hitler's Jewish victims. By this time, Roosevelt had known for more than a year that a genocide was in progress.

The War Refugee Board ran into resistance from the State Department and the British, and the Soviets refused to work with it at all. Still, it managed to evacuate a few thousand Jews through Spain, Turkey, Yugoslavia, and Switzerland. It faced its biggest challenge in the spring and summer of 1944, when the Nazis stormed into Hungary to collect the 760,000 Jews there for deportation to Auschwitz. The Slovak Jewish underground, knowing what fate awaited the Hungarian Jews, pleaded with the Allies to bomb rail lines to the death camp and the gas chambers there.

Allied bombers, by now based in Italy, hit factories at the huge Auschwitz complex in August and September that year. But all requests to destroy the gas chambers were turned down.

During the Hungarian crisis, the War Refugee Board helped get some relief supplies in to the Jews, and Swedish diplomats protected about 20,000. Partly because of these efforts, about 120,000 Jews survived in Budapest, the capital, until the Soviets arrived in February 1945. It is estimated that the Board saved as many as 200,000 Jews with evacuations, aid through the underground, diplomatic pressure, and propaganda aimed at discouraging further killing.

SOME RESISTANCE—BUT NOT ENOUGH. Within Germany and German-controlled territories, there was resistance from many quarters. During the Nazi "euthanasia" program to kill handicapped children and adults, some doctors quietly helped patients escape. Public protest did prompt Hitler to end the program. And at least two plots to overthrow Hitler were concocted by German military leaders.

At the University of Munich, a group of students calling themselves the White Rose revolted. They were led by Hans Scholl and his sister, Sophie, both former followers of Hitler who had become disillusioned. After the disaster at Stalingrad in 1943, the students printed leaflets denouncing the sacrifice of lives and declaring: "Every word that comes from Hitler's mouth is a lie. . . . His mouth is the stinking gate of hell, and his power is debased. Certainly one must conduct the battle against the National Socialist terror-state with every rational means."[1] The White

Rose uprising was short-lived. The Gestapo caught up with the Scholls, and they were quickly tried, convicted, and executed along with several other students and a professor.

In German-occupied France, the government resisted Nazi demands that French Jews be turned over, and hundreds of non-Jews in France wore the Star of David in support of their Jewish countrymen. The governments of Denmark, Italy, Hungary, Finland, Slovakia, and Bulgaria also struggled to thwart the "Final Solution." Poles chafing under Nazi rule attacked German occupying forces in August 1944, but the Germans put down the uprising in nine weeks and took brutal revenge on the rebels.

Within the ghettos and camps, Hitler's death machinery also met with resistance. The most notable uprising was in the Warsaw Ghetto, when the Nazis were moving to clear the area and send the last Warsaw Jews to their deaths. After months of preparation, the captive Jews opened fire on SS invaders on April 19, 1943, the same day the Allies opened their conference in Bermuda. Stunned, the SS men pulled out, for the moment. The vastly outmatched Jews held off the Germans for almost a month, but in the end those who survived the battle were either killed immediately or shipped to Nazi camps. Uprisings in other ghettos came to similar ends. And in the Auschwitz death camp, on October 7, 1944, some Jews who feared they would not survive to be liberated smuggled explosives out of an arms factory and blew up one of the crematoria.

But none of it was enough. The Nazi killing machine kept churning out corpses, right until the end.

THE LAST CHAPTER?

11

The forces which these defendants
represent are the darkest and most
sinister forces in society.

By their fruits we best know them.
Their acts have bathed the world
in blood and set civilization back
a century.

ROBERT H. JACKSON
PROSECUTOR, NUREMBERG

NOVEMBER 1945

The Nuremberg Trials were the first war crimes trials held in modern times. During thirteen trials Nazi leaders were charged with crimes against peace, war crimes, and crimes against humanity.

T

HE WORLD HAS CHANGED since the Nazis controlled Germany, and much of that change resulted in one way or another from the war Hitler started and the crimes he inspired.

When Adolf Hitler committed suicide, he left behind him a shattered nation, a shocked world, and the smoldering remains of violence, hate, and murder without precedent. He also left the men who believed in his programs and helped him carry them out. Now some of those men had to face judgment. The Allies assembled an International Military Tribunal in Nuremberg, Germany, and on November 20, 1945, twenty-one men were brought to trial on charges of conspiracy, crimes against peace, war crimes, and crimes against humanity. Evidence presented during the trial catalogued Nazi horrors in grisly detail. When the verdicts were handed down on September 30, 1946, only three defendants were acquitted. Of the rest, eleven were sentenced to death by hanging, and the others were given prison terms.

Hans Frank, the sadistic tyrant who ran the General Government section of Poland, tried to blame everything on the conveniently dead Hitler. Field Marshal Wilhelm Keitel and General Alfred Jodl, two of Hitler's military chiefs, claimed they had acted as honorable soldiers serving their country. Ernst Kaltenbrunner, head of the Reich Security Main Office, denied that he bore responsibility for or even knew about the mass murder of the Jews. All four were hanged at Nuremberg.

Albert Speer, the armaments minister who tried to stop Hitler from destroying Germany, went to Spandau prison for twenty years; he died in 1981. Hermann Göring, condemned to death, poisoned himself hours before he was scheduled to be hanged. Heinrich Himmler never made it to Nuremberg; he poisoned himself shortly after the Allies captured him in May 1945. Rudolf Höss, Auschwitz's commandant, was tried in Warsaw in 1947, convicted, and hanged at Auschwitz. Adolf Eichmann, organizer of the "Final Solution," was caught by Israeli agents in Argentina in 1960; he was tried in Jerusalem and was hanged in 1962. And Joseph Mengele, the doctor who cheerfully tortured and killed children at Auschwitz, fled to South America. He drowned in Brazil in 1979, and his remains were found in 1985.

A NEW WORLD ORDER. From the ashes of World War II, a new world order rose. What began as a wartime alliance became the United Nations, officially chartered in 1945. The United States and the Soviet Union emerged as the new world superpowers. The rivalry between them would dominate world politics for five decades.

When the Allies took over Germany in 1945, they faced the huge task of remaking its educational system, government, judiciary, and economy out of the mess left by the Nazis. As planned, they divided Germany into four zones to be occupied by the French, the British, the Soviets, and the Americans. Berlin, in the Soviet sector, was similarly divided. The conquerors abolished all organizations that could serve as seedbeds for the revival of militarism or Nazism.

Within months, it became clear that the Soviets intended their zone to remain separate from the other three. In 1949 the split became official. The three western zones were combined into the new democratic Federal Republic of Germany, and the Soviet zone became the German Democratic Republic, a Communist state with Soviet-style, one-party rule.

Stockpiles of a new kind of warmaking tool, atomic weapons, began to grow—and, with them, fear of nuclear war between the United States and the Soviet Union. Divided Germany became a pawn in this "Cold War" between East and West. The Western nations formed a military alliance called the North Atlantic Treaty Organization (NATO), with the Federal Republic (or West Germany) as an important member; East Germany was admitted to NATO's Soviet-led counterpart, called the Warsaw Pact.

In 1961, with Soviet backing, East German authorities built a wall topped with barbed wire around West Berlin to keep East Germans from escaping to freedom. Tens of thousands still managed to flee, and a few were killed trying. The Berlin Wall stood for almost three decades, until European communism collapsed in the bloodless revolutions of 1989. In 1990, Germany was reunited and held its first free elections as one nation since 1932.

The Nazis' genocide program galvanized Jews worldwide. Many nations had turned away Jews trying to escape Hitler, with tragic results. After the war a movement to found a Jewish state, begun in the late nineteenth century, gained enough strength to make that dream a reality. In November 1947 the United Nations approved the creation of such a state. On May 14, 1948, British control of Palestine officially ended and the State of Israel came into existence. It enacted a law authorizing Israeli agents to track down anyone who had committed crimes anywhere against the Jewish people.

A small Jewish community re-emerged in Germany, numbering about 30,000 for much of the postwar era.

IS NAZISM DEAD? The last chapter has not yet been written on Hitler's legacy. The story of Adolf Hitler and the Nazis seems to have no end.

Into the 1990s, Hitler's henchmen were still being hunted down and brought to trial for war crimes and crimes against humanity. Holocaust survivors still searched for loved ones lost fifty years earlier. Jews who had been expelled from their homes by the Nazis were still trying to reclaim their property.

And a new surge of right-wing extremism began to plague Germany as it struggled with the economic and political problems of reunification. Transforming the overstaffed Communist economy in eastern Germany into a leaner, free-market system threw a lot of people out of work. People without jobs are angry people and, as in the United States during tough times, some of those angry people looked for scapegoats.

Political parties in the Nazi mold sprang up, including one led by a former SS officer that in 1992 claimed to have 22,000 members. German neo-Nazis invoking Hitler's name attacked Jews and immigrants, killing some and leaving the country's 6 million foreign residents fearful. For the first time since Hitler was vanquished, Jews began leaving Germany to escape persecution.

There was a significant difference, though, between the racist violence racking Germany in the 1990s and the Nazi attacks of the 1920s and 1930s. This time, ordinary Germans turned out by the hundreds of thousands to protest the actions of the right-wing extremists and to demand that the government fight back. This time, Germans were acutely, painfully aware of what could happen if the majority remained silent while the rights of a minority were trampled. But the task of containing the racism and violence remained immense.

Hitler's Holocaust did not start with the gas chambers of Auschwitz. It did not start with the brutality of Kristallnacht. It began with the first tiny dent in civil liberties, the first denial of protection of one small group's rights.

Would Germany—or any other nation—let another Hitler rise? Would we recognize in time the quiet, insidious attacks on freedom? And, most important, what would we do to stop them?

Justice Robert H. Jackson, a prosecutor in the Nuremberg trials, opened his case with words that resound through the decades:

"The wrongs which we seek to condemn and punish have been so calculated, so malignant, and so devastating, that civilization cannot tolerate their being ignored because it cannot survive their being repeated."[1]

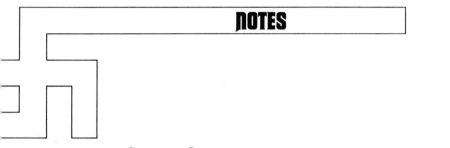

NOTES

CHAPTER ONE

1. Adolf Hitler, *Mein Kampf*, trans. Ralph Manheim (Boston: Houghton Mifflin, 1971), p. 6.
2. Hitler, p. 4.
3. Hitler, p. 21.
4. Hitler, p. 20.
5. Hitler, p. 18.
6. August Kubizek, *The Young Hitler I Knew* (Boston: Houghton Mifflin, 1955), p. 127.
7. Hitler, p. 22.
8. Hitler, p. 21.
9. Hitler, p. 56.

CHAPTER TWO

1. Adolf Hitler, *Mein Kampf*, trans. Ralph Manheim (Boston: Houghton Mifflin, 1971), p. 107.
2. Konrad Heiden, *Der Fuehrer: Hitler's Rise to Power* (Boston: Houghton Mifflin/Riverside Press Cambridge, 1944), pp. 95–96.

3. Heiden, p. 205, and Alan Bullock, *Hitler and Stalin: Parallel Lives* (New York: Alfred A. Knopf, 1992), p. 138.
4. Hitler, p. 57.

CHAPTER FOUR

1. Robert Payne, *The Life and Death of Adolf Hitler* (New York: Praeger Publishers, 1973), p. 585.
2. Payne, p. 587.

CHAPTER FIVE

1. Quoted in William L. Shirer, *The Rise and Fall of the Third Reich: A History of Nazi Germany* (New York: Simon & Schuster, 1960), p. 347.

CHAPTER SEVEN

1. Alan Bullock, *Hitler and Stalin: Parallel Lives* (New York: Alfred A. Knopf, 1992), p. 595.
2. Joe J. Heydecker and Johannes Leeb, *The Nuremberg Trial*, trans. and ed. R. A. Downie (Cleveland and New York: World Publishing Company, 1962), p. 23.
3. Bullock, p. 761.
4. Whitney R. Harris, *Tyranny on Trial: The Evidence at Nuremberg* (Dallas: Southern Methodist University Press, 1954), pp. 336–337.

CHAPTER EIGHT

1. William L. Shirer, *The Rise and Fall of the Third Reich: A History of Nazi Germany* (New York: Simon & Schuster, 1960), p. 930.

CHAPTER NINE

1. Quentin Reynolds et al., *Minister of Death: The Adolf Eichmann Story* (New York: The Viking Press, 1960), p. 177.

2. Cornelius Ryan, *The Last Battle* (New York: Simon & Schuster, 1966), p. 375.

3. Quoted in Whitney R. Harris, *Tyranny on Trial: The Evidence at Nuremberg* (Dallas: Southern Methodist University Press, 1954), p. 460.

4. Robert Payne, *The Life and Death of Adolf Hitler* (New York: Praeger Publishers, 1973), p. 589.

5. Thomas Childers, *A History of Hitler's Empire*, Audiotapes of lectures presented in Washington, D.C., April 28–29, 1990 (Dubuque, Iowa: The Teaching Company, 1992), lecture 8.

CHAPTER TEN

1. Peter Padfield, *Himmler* (New York: Henry Holt and Company, 1990), p. 429.

CHAPTER ELEVEN

1. Whitney R. Harris, *Tyranny on Trial: The Evidence at Nuremberg* (Dallas: Southern Methodist University Press, 1954), pp. 35–36.

FURTHER READING

A book of this length can offer only a glance at Adolf Hitler and the Holocaust. For readers who would like to learn more, I particularly recommend these works:

Hitler, Adolf. *Mein Kampf*. Translated by Ralph Manheim. Boston: Houghton Mifflin, 1971. Long, rambling, sometimes almost incoherent— and quite revealing.

Lifton, Robert Jay. *The Nazi Doctors: Medical Killing and the Psychology of Genocide*. New York: Basic Books, Inc., 1986. Looks hard at the question: How could they do those things? Tough reading in some passages, but worth the effort.

Reynolds, Quentin, Ephraim Katz, and Zwy Aldouby. *Minister of Death: The Adolf Eichmann Story*. New York: The Viking Press, 1960.

Rogasky, Barbara. *Smoke and Ashes: The Story of the Holocaust*. New York: Holiday House, 1988. Brief, powerful account.

Ryan, Cornelius. *The Last Battle*. New York: Simon and Schuster, 1966. An account of the final weeks before the collapse of the Third Reich, focusing on the people involved.

Speer, Albert. *Inside the Third Reich: Memoirs*. Translated by Richard and Clara Winston. New York: The Macmillan Company, 1970. An insider's view of the personalities at the top of the Nazi hierarchy. Historians dispute Speer's version of some events.

OTHER SOURCES USED IN THIS BOOK:

Astor, Gerald. *The 'Last' Nazi: The Life and Times of Dr. Joseph Mengele*. New York: Donald I. Fine, Inc., 1985.

Bullock, Alan. *Hitler and Stalin: Parallel Lives*. Alfred A. Knopf, New York: 1992.

Cameron, James. *The Making of Israel*. New York: Taplinger Publishing Company, 1977.

Childers, Thomas. *A History of Hitler's Empire*. Audiotapes of eight lectures presented in Washington, D.C., April 28 and 29, 1990. SuperStar Teachers series. Dubuque, Iowa: The Teaching Company, 1992.

Fest, Joachim C. *Hitler*. Translated by Richard and Clara Winston. New York: Harcourt Brace Jovanovich, 1974.

———. *The Face of the Third Reich: Portraits of the Nazi Leadership*. New York: Pantheon, 1970.

Fitzgibbon, Constantine. *A Concise History of Germany*. New York: The Viking Press, 1973.

"Germany and Eastern Europe Since 1945." Keesing's Research Report 8. New York: Charles Scribner's Sons, 1973.

Goebbels, Joseph. *The Goebbels Diaries, 1939–1941*. Edited and translated by Fred Taylor. New York: Putnam, 1982.

———. *The Goebbels Diaries: 1942–1943*. Edited and translated by Louis P. Lochner. Garden City, New York: Doubleday & Company, 1948.

———. *Final Entries 1945: The Diaries of Joseph Goebbels*. Translated by Richard Barry. Edited by Hugh Trevor-Roper. New York: Putnam, 1978.

Harris, Whitney R. *Tyranny on Trial: The Evidence at Nuremberg*. Dallas: Southern Methodist University Press, 1954.

Heiden, Konrad. *Der Fuehrer: Hitler's Rise to Power.* Boston: Houghton Mifflin Company/The Riverside Press Cambridge, 1944.

Heston, Leonard L., and Renate Heston. *The Medical Casebook of Adolf Hitler.* New York: Stein and Day, 1980.

Heydecker, Joe J., and Johannes Leeb. *The Nuremberg Trial.* Translated and edited by R. A. Downie. Cleveland and New York: The World Publishing Company, 1962.

Heyes, Eileen. *Children of the Swastika: The Hitler Youth.* Brookfield, CT: The Millbrook Press, 1993.

Hilberg, Raul. *The Destruction of the European Jews.* Revised and definitive edition. 3 vols. Holmes & Meier. New York, London: 1985.

Hitler, Adolf. *Hitler's Secret Book.* Translated by Salvator Attanasio. New York: Grove Press, 1961.

Kubizek, August. *The Young Hitler I Knew.* Boston: Houghton Mifflin Company, 1955.

Long, Robert Emmet, ed. *The Reunification of Germany.* The Reference Shelf, Vol. 64, No. 1. New York: The H.W. Wilson Company, 1992.

Lookstein, Haskel. *Were We Our Brothers' Keepers?* New York: Hartmore House, 1985. Reprint, New York: Vintage Books, 1988.

The Los Angeles Times, 1992 and 1993.

Padfield, Peter. *Himmler.* New York: Henry Holt, 1990.

Payne, Robert. *The Life and Death of Adolf Hitler.* New York: Praeger Publishers, 1973.

Riefenstahl, Leni (director). *Triumph of the Will (Der Triumph des Willens).* NSDAP. Distributed by Emgee Films, 1936.

Shirer, William L. *The Rise and Fall of the Third Reich: A History of Nazi Germany.* New York: Simon and Schuster, 1960.

Vandenbosch, Amry, and Willard N. Hogan. *The United Nations: Background, Organization, Functions, Activities.* New York: McGraw-Hill Book Company, 1952.

Wyman, David S. *The Abandonment of the Jews: America and the Holocaust, 1941–1945.* New York: Pantheon Books, 1984.

CHROΠOLOGY

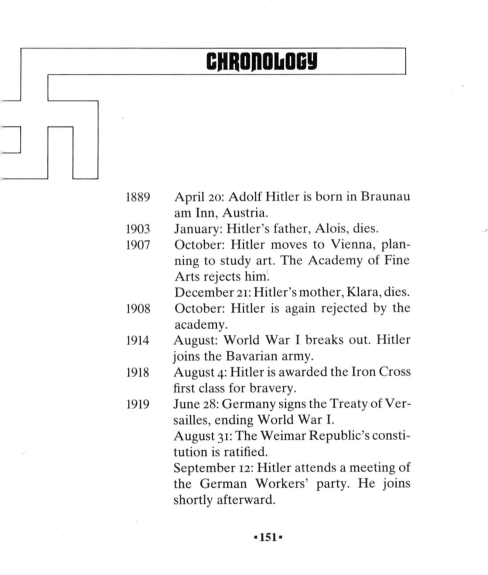

1889	April 20: Adolf Hitler is born in Braunau am Inn, Austria.
1903	January: Hitler's father, Alois, dies.
1907	October: Hitler moves to Vienna, planning to study art. The Academy of Fine Arts rejects him.
	December 21: Hitler's mother, Klara, dies.
1908	October: Hitler is again rejected by the academy.
1914	August: World War I breaks out. Hitler joins the Bavarian army.
1918	August 4: Hitler is awarded the Iron Cross first class for bravery.
1919	June 28: Germany signs the Treaty of Versailles, ending World War I.
	August 31: The Weimar Republic's constitution is ratified.
	September 12: Hitler attends a meeting of the German Workers' party. He joins shortly afterward.

1920	February 24: The party changes its name to National Socialist German Workers' party, or Nazi party.
1921	Hitler's meetings draw thousands. The Nazi party adopts a banner with a swastika.
1923	January 11: France occupies Germany's Ruhr region. Germans respond by going on strike. Devastating hyperinflation follows.
	September 24: The "Ruhr war" is halted.
	November 8: Hitler attempts a rebellion, or putsch, in a Munich beer hall. It fails, and Hitler is charged with treason.
1924	April 1–December 20: Hitler, in prison for his role in the Beer Hall Putsch, begins dictating *Mein Kampf.*
1925	First volume of *Mein Kampf* is published.
1926	Germany joins the League of Nations.
1928	May 20: The Nazi party wins 12 Reichstag seats.
1929	October: American stock market crashes, sparking worldwide depression that hits Germany hard.
1930	March: Germany begins being governed by decree, under emergency power granted in the constitution.
	September 14: Nazis win 107 Reichstag seats, becoming Germany's second-strongest party.
1931	Unemployment reaches more than 6 million. Banks collapse. Homeless people set up tent cities.
	September 18: Hitler's niece Geli, with whom he is in love, is found dead. Hitler is profoundly saddened.
1932	March 13 and April 10: Hitler challenges Paul von Hindenburg for the presidency. Hindenburg wins, but Hitler gains acceptance by the public.
	July 31: The year's third national election makes the Nazi party Germany's strongest for the first time, with 38 percent of the vote.
	November 6: Nazis win only 33 percent of the vote in another national election.
1933	January 30: Hindenburg appoints Hitler chancellor.
	February 27: The Reichstag building in Berlin is torched.
	March 5: Despite intimidation of voters, Nazis still fall short of a majority in a national election.

March 23: Reichstag passes Enabling Act, effectively making Hitler dictator.

April 7: Hitler decrees that government workers of "non-Aryan descent" must retire. The same month, limits are placed on "non-Aryan" enrollment in schools.

1934   January 26: Germany and Poland announce their ten-year Non-Aggression Pact.

January 30: The Law for Reconstruction of the Reich gives Hitler authority to change the constitution.

Schutzstaffel, or SS, and Gestapo are merged under Heinrich Himmler.

June 30: Hitler begins his purge of the Sturmabteilung, or SA.

August 2: President Paul von Hindenburg dies. Hitler declares himself Führer of the German Reich and People.

1935   January: Saarland residents vote by a 90 percent margin to rejoin Germany.

March: Hitler reveals the existence of a German Air Force, revives the draft, and announces that the German Army will expand to 500,000.

September: Nuremberg Laws, aimed at isolating Jews from non-Jews, are passed.

1936   The Four-Year Plan is established to prepare the German economy for war.

March 7: Hitler sends German troops into the demilitarized Rhineland.

July: Civil war breaks out in Spain.

November 25: Germany and Japan sign the Anti-Comintern Pact.

1937   September: The Rome-Berlin Axis is formalized.

November: Italy joins the Anti-Comintern Pact.

November 5: Hitler tells his military chiefs he plans to get more living space by force.

1938   March 12: German troops enter Austria. The Anschluss (annexation) becomes official the next day.

May: Hitler predicts that he will smash Czechoslovakia by October 1.

September 29–30: Munich Conference is held; Hitler is handed 11,000 square miles (28,490 square kilometers) of Czechoslovakia.

November 9–10: Synagogues and businesses are wrecked and dozens are murdered in the first nationally coordinated violent attack on Jews, known as Kristallnacht.

1939   January 1: The Nazis' Central Office of Jewish Emigration is established.

January 30: Hitler predicts "the destruction of the Jews in Europe."

March: The nation of Czechoslovakia no longer exists. France and Britain announce they will help Poland if it is attacked by Germany.

May: The *St. Louis* carries Jewish refugees across the Atlantic. Cuba and the U.S. refuse to let the ship land. It returns to Europe. Britain puts tight restrictions on Jewish immigration to Palestine.

May 22: Germany and Italy sign the Pact of Steel.

August 23: Germany and the Soviet Union sign the Nazi-Soviet Pact.

September 1: Hitler attacks Poland, starting World War II. Poland is conquered within three weeks.

September 3: Britain and France declare war on Germany.

1940   March 11: Germany orders that Jews' ration cards be marked with a red *J*.

April: First major Jewish ghetto, in Lodz, Poland, is established.

April 9: Hitler attacks Norway and takes over Denmark with diplomatic pressure. Norway falls by the end of June.

May 10: Hitler launches his offensive in the West, attacking Belgium and the Netherlands.

June 4: Evacuation of British troops from Dunkirk, France, is completed.

June 5: Hitler attacks France.

June 22: France signs an armistice with Germany.

August: The Luftwaffe opens its attack on England.

September 7: The Germans turn away from military targets and begin fifty-seven days of bombing London. The attack fails to open the way for invasion, Hitler's first major loss.

September 27: Germany, Italy, and Japan join in the Tripartite Pact.

October: Warsaw ghetto is established.

December: Hitler orders preparations for an invasion of the Soviet Union, to begin on May 15, 1941.

1941   June 22: Delayed by a month while helping Mussolini, Hitler launches attack on the Soviet Union.

July 31: Göring directs Heydrich to devise "a total solution to the Jewish question."

August: Hitler calls an official halt to the euthanasia program.

Summer: News of Einsatzgruppen killings is broadcast in Moscow.

September 1: Germany orders Jews over age six to wear a Jewish star with the word Jude in the center.

October 9: Hitler declares the Soviet Union beaten.

Fall: Reports of Einsatzgruppen killings appear in *The New York Times.*

December: The first Nazi death camp, at Chelmno, Poland, opens.

December 6: The Soviets counterattack against the Germans.

December 7: Japan bombs Pearl Harbor.

December 11: Hitler declares war on the U.S.

1942   January: Nazi leaders meet for a "Final Solution" conference. Their plan for genocide is formalized.

May: The Allies stage a 1,000-bomber raid on Cologne, Germany. A Jewish group in Poland gets word to the United States that 700,000 Polish Jews have been killed and concludes that an effort to kill all European Jews is in progress.

Summer: Axis powers control much of the northern and southern shores of the Mediterranean plus territory north to the Arctic Circle, west to the Atlantic Ocean, and east to the Volga River.

August: A German industrialist tells U.S. officials that the Nazis plan to wipe out Europe's Jews.

September 13: German Sixth Army attacks Stalingrad. Within two months, the Germans are surrounded by the Soviets and trapped.

Fall: British forces defeat Germans at El Alamein, Egypt.

1943   February 2: Germans surrender at Stalingrad.

April 19: Americans and British open a twelve-day conference in Bermuda to discuss handling refugees fleeing Hitler. The same day, Jews trapped in the Warsaw ghetto attack SS troops trying to clear the ghetto.

Spring: Germans are driven from Africa.

July: German offensive against the Soviets around Kursk fails within weeks.

July 10: British and Americans land on Sicily, forcing Germans to flee.

July 25: Mussolini is forced out of office and arrested.

1944   January: Roosevelt establishes the War Refugee Board to help Hitler's Jewish victims.

June 4: Allies capture Rome.

June 6: D-Day; the Allies invade the European continent at Normandy.

July 20: German officers try to kill Hitler by bringing a time bomb to his daily military conference.

July: Soviet troops liberate the death camp at Maidanek, Poland.

August: Allies liberate Paris. Germans are pushed out of the Balkans. Allied troops come within 500 miles (805 kilometers) of Berlin. An uprising in Poland is brutally put down by occupying Germans.

September 11: Americans cross the German border.

October 7: Auschwitz inmates blow up a crematorium.

October: Hitler creates the party-controlled Volkssturm to fight for the Fatherland.

November: Stalin, Churchill, and Roosevelt draw up a secret plan for occupying Germany after the war.

December 16: Hitler launches another Ardennes offensive, also known as the Battle of the Bulge. It fails.

1945   January: Hitler authorizes retreat from the Ardennes. The Soviets shatter the German line in the East.

January 17: Auschwitz has its last roll call.

February: Stalin, Churchill, and Roosevelt meet at Yalta. They repeat their demand for unconditional surrender.

April 16: Battle of Berlin begins.

April 20: Hitler celebrates his last birthday.

April 29: Hitler marries Eva Braun.

April 30: Hitler and Braun commit suicide.

May 7: Admiral Karl Dönitz, Hitler's designated successor, surrenders unconditionally to the Allies.

October 24: United Nations charter officially comes into effect.

November 20: International Military Tribunal in Nuremberg opens its trial of twenty-one Nazis.

1946   September 30: Nuremberg verdicts are handed down, acquitting only three men. The rest are sentenced to death or prison.

1947   Rudolf Höss is tried in Warsaw, convicted, and hanged at Auschwitz.

November: United Nations approves the creation of a Jewish state.

1948   May 14: The State of Israel officially comes into existence.

1949   The Federal Republic of Germany, or West Germany, and the German Democratic Republic, or East Germany, are established.

1961   August: East German authorities erect the Berlin Wall.

1960–   Adolf Eichmann is caught in Argentina, tried in Je-
62   rusalem, and hanged.

1979   Joseph Mengele drowns in Brazil; his remains are found six years later.

1989   The Berlin Wall falls.

1990   Germany is reunited and holds its first free elections as one nation since 1932.

IΠDEX

Eden, Anthony, 133
Eichmann, Adolf, 99, 123, 140
Einsatzgruppen, 96, 98, 132
Eisenhower, Dwight D., 122
El Alamein, 112

Franco, Francisco, 68
Frank, Hans, 95, 140
Frick, Wilhelm, 48

Genocide, 9, 94, 98–103, 105,
   122, 131–136, 142
German history, 12, 13, 15–16
German Workers' party, 29–
   30
Gestapo, 54, 59, 62, 73, 99,
   100
Goebbels, Joseph, 46, 62, 63,
   64, 73, 75, 123, 126
Göring, Hermann, 48, 54,
   57, 62, 63, 64, 69, 75, 85,
   98–99, 111, 112, 120–121,
   124, 140
Groener, Wilhelm, 44
Gypsies, 96, 105

Heydrich, Reinhard, 98–99
Himmler, Heinrich, 54, 62,
   63, 64, 69, 98, 99, 114, 121,
   124, 140
Hindenburg, Paul von, 43,
   46–48, 50, 56
Hitler, Adolf, 10, 18, 25, 42,
   63, 66, 118, 125
   Anschluss and, 69–70
   as artist, 22–24
   assassination plot, 115
   becomes chancellor, 47
   Beer Hall Putsch, 33–34
   birth of, 19
   Blood Purge and, 55–56
   death of, 126
   education of, 20, 21

family of, 19–23
Final Solution and, 96,
   98, 99, 105
imprisonment of, 34–36
last days in bunker, 119–
   120, 123–125
Lebensraum and, 35,
   67, 79
marriage of, 125
*Mein Kampf (My Strug-
   gle)*, 27, 35–36, 41, 65,
   77, 91
Munich Agreement,
   72–73
Nazi party and, 11, 29–
   32, 36, 37, 39, 44, 46–
   48, 50, 59
racial views of, 11, 22,
   24, 35–36, 54, 56, 57,
   79, 82, 93, 96, 98, 126
rearmament and, 57–58
religion and, 19, 20, 80,
   82
Sudetenland and, 70, 72
Hitler, Alois, 19–21
Hitler, Alois, Jr., 20
Hitler, Klara, 20–22, 46
Hitler, Paula, 20
Hitler Youth, 54
Holocaust, 93–103, 105, 131–
   136, 142
Höss, Rudolf, 101–103, 123,
   140

Jackson, Robert H., 137, 144
Jews, 9, 11–13, 48, 54–56, 70,
   73–75, 79, 92, 93–103, 97,
   105, 130–136, 142, 143
Jodl, Alfred, 140

Kaltenbrunner, Ernst, 120,
   140
Keitel, Wilhelm, 140